Surrogate Motherhood

SURROGATE MOTHERHOOD

The Ethics of Using Human Beings

◆

THOMAS A. SHANNON

CROSSROAD ◆ NEW YORK

1989
The Crossroad Publishing Company
370 Lexington Avenue, New York, N.Y. 10017

Printed in the United States of America
Library of Congress Cataloging-in-Publication Data

Shannon, Thomas A. (Thomas Anthony), 1940–
    Surrogate motherhood : the ethics of using human beings / Thomas
A. Shannon.
        p.   cm.
    Bibliography: p.
    Includes index.
    ISBN 0-8245-0899-8
    1. Surrogate motherhood—Moral and ethical aspects. 2. Surrogate
mothers—Legal status, laws, etc.—United States. I. Title.
HQ759.5.S53 1988
306.8'743—dc19   88-25671
                                                                CIP

To JoAnn Manfra
Chair, Department of Humanities, WPI
In gratitude for her friendship
and continual encouragement

Contents

Introduction

The case of Mary Beth Whitehead and William and Elizabeth Stern guaranteed that few people would be unaware of the reality of surrogate motherhood as well as the multiple problems associated with it. This particular case presented almost all of the negative possibilities associated with its practice. While the end result was that the Sterns indeed had a baby biologically related to William Stern, the means to that end—as well as others yet to be discovered—proved to be exceptionally problematic for many.

The Supreme Court of New Jersey recognized these problems in its determination that surrogacy is a form of child selling and buying, that the natural mother has rights, and that surrogacy contracts are illegal. While all eagerly awaited this decision, many did not like the conclusion the court came to. While obviously neither a federal case nor binding on the other states, the case surely sets a precedent and will stand as a landmark case.

Yet problems and issues remain. For example, the desire—and quest—for a child is a powerful one. Many know individuals with fertility problems and have suffered with them to some extent. Studies of such couples reveal tremendous frustration and feelings of inferiority. Indeed, many seem driven in their quest for a child of their own. The origin of this drive—whether genetically based or culturally conditioned—is unknown. Yet for some, the meaning of marriage and self-identity hinges on this reproductive ability. Obviously we are confronted with a most significant biosocial reality and we really have little grasp of its basis, although we are certainly aware of its implications.

Adoption has been the traditional means by which the experience of childlessness has been resolved. While not a completely satisfactory solution to a couple's desire to "have a child of their own," nonetheless they had a child and could fullfill many of their desires and hopes. The artificial insemination of the wife with her husband's semen proved to be another solution to some male infertility problems. Successful insemination in this manner gave the couple a child biologically related to both. Artificial insemination with donor semen established a pregnancy by bypassing the husband, though frequently his semen would be added to the donor semen. Thus the resulting child was clearly related biologically to the mother.

In essence, surrogacy is the reversal of artificial insemination by donor. Here the wife has the infertility problem while the husband is fertile. To resolve this problem, another woman is inseminated with the husband's semen and then the child is relinquished to the couple after birth. Thus the husband is the biological father while the wife has no genetic relation to the child.

While this practice clearly resolves a couple's childlessness, various problems are raised by this practice which I would like to examine in this book. I will do this by setting contexts in which the practice of surrogacy can be critically examined and on the basis of such frameworks draw conclusions—negative ones in my judgment—about the practice of surrogacy.

In one sense, surrogacy is a variation on the practice of the use of humans and their bodies for various purposes. Thus we have the practice of blood donation (and often selling), organ donation (and sometimes selling), participation in research protocols (sometimes for a fee), and of wet nursing (generally for a fee). All of these practices reveal perceptions about the body and the limits to its use. Thus I review these practices to articulate thematic concerns raised in discussing them. Additionally, various understandings about coercion, alienation, and the family are also significant issues associated with surrogacy. While there is a vast literature on each of these topics—and frequently an extremely disputed one—there are themes and practices worth examining. My purpose here is to highlight certain key questions and issues so that these dimensions associated with surrogacy can be more clearly thought through.

As various individuals have discussed the practice of surrogacy, a number of key questions on the social and ethical aspects of surrogacy have arisen. I identify and present these positive and negative aspects to establish a solid basis for drawing conclusions about the practice of surrogacy. I think this type of thorough review of the main issues is imperative to situate the ethical questions correctly. Additionally, a growing regulatory tradition and set of case law precedents have developed over the past decade. While it is impossible—because of extremely rapid developments in this field—to be absolutely current in this discussion, a review of the regulations and cases available as of this printing is important because trends and precedents can be shown and new direction for both practice and research established.

Finally, I will draw all these materials together into an argument against the practice of surrogacy, especially as it is practiced now. I think we must see surrogacy as a whole and not focus only on one or two issues such as commercialization (which is easily solved by permitting no fees) or problems with the form of the contract (again an easily solvable legal issue). The overarching issue is surrogacy as a practice or an institution within our culture and society. What are we saying about ourselves and our children if we regularize such a practice, regardless of how well the contract is drawn? Thus, in my judgment, the key issue is the totality of the arguments against surrogacy that mitigate against its practice. I am not convinced that any one particular argument against surrogacy can win the debate—though some arguments are clearly better and stronger than others—but the total weight of all of them strongly argues that this is a bad idea and an even worse policy or practice.

I began this book with a negative intuition against surrogacy. I conclude it with a negative argument against its practice. In the process of this I have learned that some issues are not as important as others. Coercion, for example, is not a particularly useful concept, but undue influence is. Risk factors must be carefully defined before one can factor them in. Other aspects remain as elusive as ever. What is natural and to what extent, if any, is it binding? How far do reproductive rights extend? Does freedom mean the capacity to do anything within our power or rights? The fact that our culture has no adequate or even minimal answer to these questions complicates further the resolution of surrogacy.

Yet while these traditional and profound questions continue to plague us, other concepts are at hand and can form the basis of a coherent argument against surrogacy. Thus while there is a certain conceptual "untidiness" at a deeper level, there is, I submit, enough conceptual consensus to see us through an adequate and appropriate analysis of the practice of surrogacy.

·1·

The Technologies of Surrogate Mothering

In 1923 J. B. S. Haldane, a leading geneticist, projected the following future scenario in a lecture to the Heretics Club in Cambridge:

> It was in 1951 that Dupont and Schwarz produced the first ectogenetic child. . . . Dupont and Schwarz obtained a fresh ovary from a woman who was the victim of an aeroplane accident, and kept it living in their medium for five years. They obtained several eggs from it and fertilized them successfully, but the problem of the nutrition and support of the embryo was more difficult, and was only solved in the fourth year. Now that the technique is fully developed, we can take an ovary from a woman, and keep it growing in a suitable fluid for as long as twenty years, producing a fresh ovum each month, of which 90 percent can be fertilized, and the embryos grown successfully for nine months, and then brought out into the air.
>
> As we know ectogenesis is now universal, and in this country less than 30 percent of children are now born of woman.[1]

Although surely influenced by the strong eugenics movement of his day, and while probably poking a little fun at those who took the movement too seriously, Haldane was also quick to admit that the the traditional family has some points in its favor and that a minimal, but comforting, link to nature in this artificial environment was provided by chemically stimulating lactation. However, he also indicated that the benefits outweighed the costs:

1

The small proportion of men and women who are selected as ancestors for the next generation are so undoubtedly superior to the average that the advance in each generation in any single respect, from the increased output of first-class music to the decreased convictions for theft, is very startling. Had it not been for ectogenesis there can be little doubt that civilization would have collapsed within a measurable time owing to the greater fertility of the less desirable members of the population in almost all countries.[2]

Such eugenic applications were carried a degree further by Adlous Huxley when, nine years later, he wrote *Brave New World*. In this dystopia, Huxley described the new technologies that allowed the development of custom-designed populations to ensure social stability. At the heart of this were two biological processes: Bokanovsky's Process and Podsnap's Technique. The former allowed the manufacture of up to ninety-six, but on average seventy-two, pairs of identical twins from a single ovary with gametes from the same male. The latter accelerated the process of ripening.

They could make sure of at least a hundred and fifty mature eggs within two years. Fertilize and bokanovskify—in other words, multiply by seventy-two—and you get an average of nearly eleven thousand brothers and sisters in a hundred and fifty batches of identical twins, all within two years of the same age.[3]

While clearly in the dystopic tradition and a satire on the eugenics movement of his day, it is nonetheless remarkable how accurate Huxley was with respect to the technologies he described. Many of them are in use today, excepting of course the complete exogenic process—quaintly referred to as decanting—and the total control over the genetic code. And, in contrast to Haldane, Huxley underscores the dark side of genetic control, by illustrating the loss of identity and totalitarianism.

But concern about artificial reproduction and surrogate mothers is not limited to scientists or scholars. Religious traditions also discuss the use of surrogates.

> Abram's wife Sarai had born him no child, but she had an Egyptian maidservant named Hagar. So Sarai said to Abram, "Listen, now! Since Yahweh has kept me from having children, go to my slave-girl. Perhaps I shall get children through her." Abram agreed to what Sarai had said.
>
> Thus after Abram had lived in the land of Canaan for ten years Sarai took Hagar her Egyptian slave-girl and gave her to Abram as his wife. He went to Hagar and she conceived.[4]

The use of female slaves as surrogates was acceptable in Mesopotamian law and evidently was adopted by many of the Semitic peoples. However, such a practice was not without its difficulties.

> And once she knew she conceived, her mistress counted for nothing in her eyes. Then Sarai said to Abram, "May this insult to me come home to you! It was I who put my slave-girl into your arms but now she knows that she has conceived, I count for nothing in her eyes. Let Yahweh judge between me and you." "Very well," Abram said to Sarai, "your slave-girl is at your disposal. Treat her as you think fit." Sarai accordingly treated her so badly that she ran away from her.[5]

And, as Jacob discovered, sometimes the practice could lead to very complex—and demanding—familial obligations. Jacob wanted to marry Rachel but her father deceitfully arranged that Jacob marry Leah, her older sister. But after another seven years of labor, Jacob was also permitted to marry Rachel. Then, because "Yahweh saw that Leah was neglected, . . . he opened her womb, while Rachel remained barren."[6] After Leah had two children, Rachel became jealous and gave Jacob her slave-girl Bilhah with whom Jacob had two children. Then Leah, who experienced barrenness again, took her slave-girl Zilpah and gave her to Jacob with whom he had two more children. Later, Jacob had three more children with Leah and yet another with Rachel.[7]

While such complications may not have been the norm, nonetheless the possibility of problems arises quickly, especially in the context of the practice of polygamy. Evidently social harmony was not necessarily the goal of such practices.

Ancient and modern sources discuss the impact and implications of alternative birth practices and birth technologies on various populations and social systems. Our age is characterized by having available to it many birth technologies that others speculated about or imagined. Let us now examine these technologies as a way of entering into the study of the contemporary practice of surrogate mothering.

CONTEMPORARY BIRTH TECHNOLOGIES

In Vitro Fertilization

After the development of the techniques of artificial insemination and the technology of sperm preservation through freezing, the most critical development in the area of birth technologies was in vitro fertilization (IVF). And the brief, matter of fact letter by Steptoe and Edwards in the *Lancet*[8] announcing the birth of the first IVF baby revealed nothing of the history or complexity of the process that resulted in the birth of Louise Brown in 1978.

The earliest attempts at external fertilization can be traced back to the 1890s when research was done on marine animals. This work was transferred to mice and rabbits in the 1930s,[9] and in 1947 M. Chang reported the fertilization and development of rabbit ova in vitro.[10] This work represented the culmination of a century of research on reproduction, beginning with the discovery of the human egg in 1827 by Karl Ernst von Baer, the identification of the development of sperm in 1847, and progress, in the mid 1900s, in understanding of the female reproductive cycle.

The role of two hormones is of particular importance in IVF. The follicle-stimulating hormone (or FSH) stimulates the development of eggs and the lutenizing hormone (or LH) functions to mature the eggs. To ensure the harvesting of an adequate number of eggs to be fertilized externally, FSH and LH are administered to stimulate the development and release of several eggs (also known as superovulation) and to ensure that these eggs are sufficiently mature. The eggs are harvested through the technique of laparoscopy in which a small incision is made below the navel and a microscope, fiber-optic lamp, and catheter are inserted to locate the eggs, which are then drawn into a tube and removed.

Several problems then need to be overcome. First is the development of a fluid in which the eggs can be maintained until they are fertilized. The second is facilitating the process of capacitation during which the sperm undergo a chemical transformation which enables them to fertilize the egg. Part of the sperm's head is shed resulting in movement and a capacity to penetrate the ovum. Third, a culture needs to be developed in which the fertilized egg can be maintained and nourished until implantation.[11]

Having successfully resolved all these problems, the major obstacle has to be faced.

> The greatest difficulty to be overcome before human IVF can be generally available for the treatment of infertility is the inability to achieve uterine implantation of the transfered embryo. Steptoe and Edwards and others have attempted over 70 unsuccessful implantations of embryos derived from hormonally primed cycles and resulting from fertilization in vitro of the recipient's egg by her husband's sperm.[12]

The two primary concerns are the synchronizing of the development of the uterus with the development of the fertilized egg and identifying the optimal location for the placement of the fertilized egg. Then the egg must implant itself in the uterine wall and be successful in its further development.

Given these problems and all the complications that can arise, it is not surprising that IVF has low levels of success. A major study reports that of 1,110 embryo transfers only 184 led to pregnancies. This is a success rate of 17 percent and is based on reported data from 13 international clinics. Since the success rate of natural fertilization is 45 percent, IVF is only about 40 percent as efficient as the customary[13] method.[14] Yet for many, IVF remains the only hope of either establishing a pregnancy or of ensuring that the embryo is made up of the genetic material of the parents.

Embryo Transfer

Embryo transfer (ET) can be consequent to either in vitro or in vivo conception achieved either through artificial insemination or customary intercourse. After the pregnancy is established, the embryo is loosened from the uterine lining and withdrawn via a catheter. After examination, the embryo is then reimplanted into the the prepared uterus of another woman.[15]

Such a procedure solves two problems. First is the case of the woman who can conceive but experiences frequent miscarriages. She and her partner can conceive a child customarily and then have the embryo transferred to a surrogate who can carry it to term for them. The second case is that of a woman who cannot conceive because of some pathology. A surrogate can become impregnated and the embryo transferred to the first woman who can then carry it to term.

Because the technique does not require laparoscopy, it requires neither anesthesia nor drugs. It is safer and less expensive. Also the embryo stays outside the uterus for a far shorter period than with traditional IVF. Problems are presented by the possibility of an ectopic pregnancy or failure to flush the embryo from the uterus of the woman who is to conceive.

Embryo Freezing

Although Edwards and Steptoe had tried, in connection with their IVF program, to freeze embryos as early as 1977, they soon abandoned their efforts after failing to have them develop after thawing out. In 1980 three Australian physicians—Carl Wood, Alan Trounson, and John Leeton—developed a successful technique. They approached the Queen Victoria Hospital Ethics Committee and asked permission to freeze, store, thaw, and implant embryos. The justification was that this procedure was better than destroying the embryos or using them for research. The committee agreed and soon a program was initiated.[16]

Although the embryos could be frozen and thawed, the first attempts at implantation were unsuccessful and it was not until 1984 that the first frozen embryo baby was born. The process soon became widespread and is being used in programs in England, Australia, and the United States. As of December 1984 there were approximately 50 frozen embryos at the program at the

University of Southern California.[17] And in Australia, 130 embryos have been frozen and 45 implanted, resulting in 7 pregnancies and 2 miscarriages.[18]

Thus, while the freezing technique seems to be established and scientifically accepted, the success rate is not yet equal to that of IVF. Nonetheless, the method provides an interim solution to the problem of what to do with fertilized eggs that have no immediate use.

Egg Donation

Hormonal stimulation to increase the yield of eggs harvested during the laparoscopy allows women to do what men have long been able to do: donate their genetic material. In addition to the options of fertilizing all the eggs, implanting some and freezing the others, the woman can also donate an egg to a woman incapable of producing an egg but capable of maintaining a pregnancy. Should a woman not already undergoing laparoscopy choose to be an egg donor, she would have to undergo hormonal stimulation and laparoscopy specifically for that purpose. This procedure is in use and may become as widespread as the other technologies.[19]

Summary

Together with the traditional use of artificial insemination either with donor semen or the semen of the spouse of the couple contracting with a surrogate, these technologies offer a wide range of opportunities for establishing conception and implantation. They ensure that half or all of the genetic material of the embryo comes from either or both of the social parents. Thus, if the husband of a couple had a genetic disease and the wife were unable to carry a pregnancy, she could either have eggs removed and fertilized by a donor and then have them implanted in the surrogate or herself be artificially inseminated by a donor, have the pregnancy established, and then transfer the embryo to a surrogate. Alternatively, if the wife of a couple could not produce eggs but could carry a pregnancy, either an egg could be obtained from a donor, fertilized in vitro, and implanted in the wife or a surrogate could be artificially inseminated by the husband of the couple and the embryo transferred to the wife.

In all of these cases the embryo has a genetic relation to one of the members of the couple. It is also possible for a couple to obtain a frozen embryo, have a surrogate carry the pregnancy to term, and then take the infant.

The biological possibilities are limited only by the technical capabilities. We have completed a process begun when contraception separated sex and reproduction. We have now succeeded in separating reproduction from sex. Thus it is possible to become the parent of a child who has a genetic relation to one or both of the social parents when they have neither engaged in customary intercourse nor carried the pregnancy.

AN OVERVIEW

The technical possibilities which have given rise to the possibility of surrogate motherhood have also raised a host of ethical, social, and legal problems. While we have, for example, the experience of blended families as the result of death and remarriage or divorce and remarriage, the use of a surrogate creates a different type of blended family. And while we have the experience of wet nurses, surrogacy has pushed this experience back one step and allowed a woman to be a birth mother only. These new relations need to be clarified.

Also the issue of "ownership" of the semen, egg, and fertilized egg—whether in vitro, in vivo, or frozen—presents a complex range of problems, both legal and ethical. The issue of who exercises rights over this material and for how long is a critical one, especially in the case of a frozen embryo. A peculiar ethical/philosophical problem arises when one considers the moral status of the frozen embryo. What is the frozen embryo while frozen? It is clearly in a state of suspended animation—a soul on ice, if you will—but is it a person and what rights does it have?

Surrogacy also presents analagous relations to other situations: organ donations, wet nurses, research subjects, and blood donors. Should surrogacy simply be considered another form of donation of body parts or should a fee be charged, as many desire?

Finally, what policies should be set, if any, and by whom? Presently the whole area of noncoital reproduction is essentially unregulated, except for federal guidelines restricting some form of research on the fetus and prohibiting any public funding relating to the new birth technologies.

In the remainder of this book, I will examine many of the problems raised by surrogate motherhood and attempt to present some perspective on the social, ethical, and legal consequences of this new mode of parenting.

·2·

Moral Analogues
to Surrogate Mothering

Developing a moral analysis of any topic is always difficult. Commitment to a particular method of analysis guarantees that critical issues will be overlooked and that some relevant concepts may be dismissed. If one applies abstract moral concepts to the topic, the richness of the context is lost. And if one looks only to the context or outcomes, relevant moral dimensions may be dismissed.

As a way around some of these difficulties, I will conduct my analysis at first indirectly. I will begin by describing issues that are analogous to surrogate mothering as a way of establishing a frame of reference. Here I will look at the situations of blood donation, organ donation, fees for participating in research, and wet nurses.

Next, I will describe various issues concerning families and parenthood as a way of understanding possible social arrangements. This will help us understand the range of options available and facilitate our locating surrogacy within a social context.

Finally, I will examine several moral issues that I think are both directly related to the surrogacy issue and are in congruence with the previously discussed topics. Here I will focus on alienation, manipulation, and coercion.

I hope that this method of analysis by indirection will provide both a context and basis for the moral analysis of surrogate mothering. By relating surrogacy to other analogous practices I hope to provide a reasonable basis for my moral evaluation and to illuminate further the moral reality of surrogate motherhood.

THE SELLING OF BLOOD

The debate over how to obtain blood and blood products has split over two self-evident alternatives: selling blood or donating it. Because this debate involves the disposal of a body product, it provides a useful analogy with surrogacy. Additionally, Titmuss has done us the service of providing a major, if not definitive, analysis of the two methods of obtaining blood.[1] Titmuss studied comparative methods of obtaining blood in the United States and England, with brief references to the methods of other countries. Although sixteen years old and not reflecting contemporary U.S. practice, the book still raises serious questions.

In the United States, the majority of blood was obtained by methods involving cash payment or repayment to a blood bank. About half of the blood came from two major groups which Titmuss calls the Responsibility Fee Donor and the Family Credit Donor.[2] The former represents a group which has been lent blood for an operation and then must pay for the blood in cash, replace the blood themselves through donations, or have others replace the blood for them. The Family Credit Donation plan is a system in which one predeposits in a blood bank or plan so this person and his or her family has blood available to them if necessary. The next largest largest source of blood is the paid donor who, in Titmuss's study, provided 29 percent of all blood collected.[3]

In the United States, only about 3 percent of blood collected came from voluntary donors.[4] However, when we look at England the case is dramatically different.

> Virtually all donors in Britain and donors in some systems in a number of other European countries fall into this category [the voluntary donor].[5]

This stark contrast provided the basis for moral and social analysis for the two systems. I will summarize several of Titmuss's findings and his concerns about obtaining blood through payments.

First, an assumption was made, both in the United States and

Britain, that paying donors would increase both their number and frequency of visits. Second, such commercialization of the system would ensure that supply would keep up with demand.[6] Third, there was

> the assumption that as standards of living rose and societies became richer . . . the commercialization of blood will decline.[7]

In response to these suggestions, Titmuss laconically responds: "Such theories are not born out by the experience of the United States, Germany, or Japan."[8] Thus in one form or another, with the conspicuous exception of Great Britain, most blood is obtained through some sort of payment or incentive program. Titmuss identifies four major concerns with such commercialization of obtaining blood.

First is the conflict of interest between the one who is selling blood and the truth about his or her health.

> The paid seller of blood is confronted and, moreover, usually knows that he is confronted with a personal conflict of interests. To tell the truth about himself, his way of life and his relationships may limit his freedom to sell his blood on the market. Because he desires money and is not seeking in this particular act to affirm a sense of belonging he thinks primarily of his own freedom; he separates his freedom from other people's freedom.[9]

While many of the abuses Titmuss refers to in this context, such as the uncritical use of drug users and street people as donors, have been stopped, there still are individuals who qualify as professional donors—individuals in plasmapheresis programs—who need to follow a fairly strict health routine and there are all the other individuals who need to replace blood either with their own or with that of friends or relatives. Monetary factors can ensure that the conflict of interest remains.

Second, Titmuss expresses concerns about the possible generalization of the selling of blood.

> If blood is considered in theory, in law, and is treated in practice as a trading commodity then ultimately human hearts,

kidneys, eyes and other organs of the body may also come to be treated as commodities to be bought and sold in the marketplace.[10]

Titmuss's concern is the generalization of the practice of selling body parts which may set in motion a possibly problematic practice.

If dollars or pounds exchange for blood then it may be morally acceptable for a myriad of other human activities and relationships also to exchange for dollars and pounds.[11]

Thus the continued practice of buying and selling blood may make it easier to mainline the selling of other body parts or to commercialize other relations.

Third, once one begins to sell blood, then one has to deal with the realities of the market.

If blood as a living human tissue is increasingly bought and sold as an article of commerce and profit accrues from such transactions then it follows that the laws of commerce must, in the end, prevail.[12]

Such commercialization will further lead to submission to the "same laws of restraint and warranty as those that obtain in the buying and selling of consumption goods."[13] This means that choices about where one can obtain blood can be limited and that malpractice suits can be more easily justified.

The fourth is the impact of such commercialization elsewhere.

Ethical considerations are, as we said earlier, also endangered when scientific, technological and economic considerations are uppermost. Concrete illustration of this danger—particularly to captive donors—are increasingly being provided by those engaged in the world of medical science.[14]

Titmuss wrote this at a time of concern about the ethical use of humans in medical research. Consequent to discovering many ethical problems in the conducting of research in the United States, a presidential commission was established to examine this and other emerging ethical aspects of medicine.[15] But Titmuss was also concerned with the impact of such practices on the critical value of altruism.

> What we do suggest, however, is that the ways in which society organizes and structures its social institutions—and particularly its health and welfare systems—can encourage or discourage the altruism in man; such systems can foster integration or alienation; they can allow the "theme of the gift" (to recall Mauss's words)—of generosity toward strangers—to spread among and between social groups and generations. This we further suggest, is an aspect of freedom in the twentieth century which, compared with the emphasis on consumer choice in material acquisitiveness, is insufficiently recognized. It is indeed little understood how modern society, technical professional, large-scale organized society, allows for practical opportunities for ordinary people to articulate giving in morally practical terms outside their own network of family and personal relationships.[16]

Thus, by commercializing blood and other activities of life, altruism decreases, intergenerational relations atrophy, and humans find themselves more and more alone. Such decreased opportunities for altruism—decreased even for those who wish to donate blood—increase the opportunities for making routine human relations economic transactions that are subject to all that the market brings with it.

Conflicts of interest, the implications of the generalization of the practice of selling blood, the commercialization of relationships, and the decrease in altruism encouraged by social policy are substantive ethical concerns raised by Titmuss in his study. While the evidence and arguments he developed to critique the policy of selling blood are not unassailable, nonetheless they are quite compelling. Of critical importance are the ethical and empirical conclusions he draws from his study.

> From our study of the private market in blood in the United States we have concluded that the commercialization of blood and donor relationships represses the expression of altruism, erodes the sense of community, lowers scientific standards,

limits both personal and professional freedoms, sanctions the making of profits in hospitals and clinical labratories, legalizes hostility between doctor and patient, subjects critical areas of medicine to the laws of the marketplace, places immense social costs on those least able to bear them—the poor, the sick and the inept—increases the danger of unethical behaviour in various sectors of medical science and practice, and results in situations in which proportionately more and more blood is supplied by the poor, the unskilled, the unemployed, Negroes and other low income groups and categories of exploited human populations of high blood yielders. Redistribution in terms of blood and blood products from the poor to the rich appears to be one of the dominant effects of the American blood banking systems.

Moreover, on four testable non-ethical criteria the commercialized blood market is bad. In terms of economic efficiency it is highly wasteful of blood; shortages, chronic and acute, characterize the demand and supply position and make illusory the concept of equilibrium. It is administratively inefficient and results in more bureaucratization and much greater administrative, accounting and computer overheads. In terms of price per unit of blood to the patient (or consumer) it is a system which is five to fifteen times more costly than the voluntary system in Britain. And, finally, in terms of quality, commercial markets are much more likely to distribute contaminated blood; the risks for the patient of disease and death are substantially greater. Freedom from disability is inseparable from altruism.[17]

Such conclusions are all the more frightening because of the solid reasoning and empirical evidence behind them. Clearly, in the case of the commercialization of the blood supply in the United States the results have been detrimental to society, the sick, and the poor.

HUMAN ORGAN PROCUREMENT

Another analogous context for thinking about surrogate mothers is the procurement of human organs for transplantation. While this stands in dramatic contrast to blood procurement in that the giving of organs is truly a voluntary act, the experience has been one of continual shortage of organs. Thus a study of organ procurement will provide an example of a voluntary practice and will illuminate other ethical and policy concerns.

Beginning in the early 1950s with limited success, organ transplantation has become routine and successful. Improvements in technology, surgical procedures, and the use of drugs to suppress the immune system have all contributed to our acceptance of organ transplantation as another standard practice in contemporary medicine. Yet in spite of these successes, "The Centers for Disease Control has [sic] estimated that no more than 15 per cent of the 20,000 persons who might serve as donors actually do so."[18] This is the case even though between 6000 and 10,000 persons are being maintained on dialysis while awaiting a kidney for transplantation and another 4000 are in need of corneal transplantations.

Such a gap between need and supply is somewhat puzzling. The Uniform Anatomical Gift Act, first proposed in 1968 and adopted by almost all states within a year, essentially removed all legal obstacles that would prevent anyone who had attained the age of majority from being an organ donor. Most assumed this act would dramatically increase the supply of available organs, but such was not the case. Several reasons have been given. One, offered by the director of a Procurement Center, suggests that the major issue is to train health care professionals to identify potential donors and refer them to the procurement network.[19] This director sees the issue primarily as a pragmatic one with better training providing the solution. Others, however, see the problem in ethical terms.

> The organ retrieval process presents participating health professionals with at least three moral problems. First of all, ... during retrieval, the donor's welfare no longer provides the rationale for these aggressive procedures. Secondly, the organ recovery process seems to violate a more general respect for persons, which obligates us to treat human beings as ends in themselves rather than as mere means to other ends. Thirdly, organ retrieval may be viewed as being disrespectful to the dead. Our cultural and moral traditions demand that we respect not only recently dead bodies but also graves that are centuries old.[20]

These concerns define the problem as a professional one: the onus is on the professional to identify a potential donor and then to take steps to enlist that individual. But few means are given the professionals to overcome these priorities.

Other solutions address the donor. The system in place currently is referred to as an "opt in" system in which the individual must actively choose to become a donor. While the Uniform Anatomical Gift Act removed legal obstacles to becoming a donor, nonetheless the individual must still choose to do so. Another proposal is the "opt out" system in which all individuals would, at their death, be considered donors unless they actively chose not to. Such a system presupposes most individuals would not object to donating bodily parts—and public opinion polls seem to indicate this. The problem is most people do nothing about becoming a donor which is further complicated by the reluctance of professionals to enter into the process. A third system, in place in New York and other states, is the required request system. This policy requires that professionals ask the families of potential donors if their relative can be a donor. The apparent advantages of this policy are that it avoids the seeming crudeness of the "opt out" system, may help overcome professional reluctance to ask potential donors, and will not single out any particular family. The hope is that such a policy will have an educational effect and that people will become more sensitive to the need for transplantation.

The systems currently in place are essentially voluntary. An organ donor is a genuine donor. The only reward is the benefit of having acted altruisticaly. Yet, as noted, the need far outstrips the supply. To remedy this situation, yet another strategy is proposed: selling one's organs. Such a system would, it is argued, have three major benefits. First, the supply of organs would be increased.

> Common sense—backed by extensive data on the relationship between economics and human behavior—suggests that many persons who would not donate their organs altruistically might sell those organs for a price.[21]

Second, the need for organs from living donors may be decreased.

if the sale of organs were restricted to organs removed only after the donor had died, with the altruistic system supplying organs from living individuals *and* from deceased individuals, the larger supply generated from deceased donors through the market system might reduce the need for organ removal from living donors.[22]

Finally, there might be a therapeutic benefit in that the success rate of organ transplants might rise.

Because preferred donors are not always available either from live or from cadaver sources, doctors often must resort to less preferred donors. The larger supply of donors under a market system, even if the system were limited to cadavers and excluded live donors, would provide doctors with greater choice and thereby would enhance the possibility of obtaining organs which have less probability of being rejected.[23]

After proposing this system, the author then responds to pragmatic and ethical objections to this market approach. *Pragmatically*, there might be a decrease in free organs, some patients may not be able to pay, and the quality of organs may decrease. In response, Brams argues that a decrease in free organs is a small price to pay for an overall increase in supply, that other forms of health care are not denied to people who can afford them because others cannot, and that careful physical examinations will solve the quality problem.[24] *Ethically*, a market system which increases the supply of organs is ethically superior to a voluntary system which has produced only shortages. Second, a person who sells an organ could be doing so for altruistic reasons, for example, to satisfy family needs or, perhaps, to provide an education for one's self or family members. Finally,

we must remember that the other necessary commodities such as food, shelter, and medication are currently supplied primarily through a market system, with relatively few ethical objections being raised. Why should we, as a society, view the sale of human organs differently? If it is because the prospect of financial reward may pressure an individual into making a choice which is not truly free, then we should take notice that most individuals make important decisions throughout their lives which reflect a need for money, yet such decisions are generally regarded as being freely made.[25]

Other critiques of a restraint on the sale of organs are as follows. First, the supply of organs may not be inelastic—donors may not wish to sell their bodies at any price. Although we have deep emotional and spiritual attitudes to the body, these may cease after death. Additionally, other feelings about the cadaver may be weakening. Changing perceptions about the role of the body in contemporary medicine may also help reinforce such changed attitudes. Finally, this argument only applies to dead bodies and says nothing about the willingnes of living individuals to sell their body parts.[26]

Second, someone willing to sell might be induced to donate organs if the system were voluntary. The argument against this is twofold. First, since, for living donors, there is a risk to donating, more inducement than altruism is needed. Second, as just mentioned, religious and emotional attitudes toward cadavers tend to discourage relatives from donating.

The third argument against the market approach is that the quality of organs will decrease. Such problems can be resolved by utilizing the time between sale and delivery to do a thorough medical history or to require the seller to submit to periodic checkups.[27]

Let us now examine other arguments against such a system. After recognizing the significance of the arguments of increasing the supply of organs and the traditional liberty over one's body, George Annas notes that there is an instinctive social reaction against permitting market in organs. Interestingly enough, Annas moves quickly from recognizing that this reaction may come from an ancient reaction against cannibalism to arguing that today this sentiment is "animated by a more sophisticated refusal to accept a symbolic and highly visible form of exploitation of the poor."[28] The fear of exploitation of the poor was previously sounded in 1970 by D. Hamburger, then president of the Transplantation Society. He feared the dangers of possible blackmail, unfair ad-

vantage being taken of the poor and other vulnerable populations, and the possibility of coercion's being used in countries
where personal liberty was not highly valued.[29]

The theme of voluntary consent is an important one. In England, for example, an amendment to the Human Tissue Act
which would establish an "opt out" system was rejected because
of the "deeply ingrained belief that such gifts of life should be
the product of a voluntary affirmative act."[30] George Annas con-
curs with the emphasis on voluntarism.

> There are many arguments against a market in organs in-
> cluding a dilution of altruism, a less dependable product, the
> pricing of a priceless gift, the tendency to view human body
> parts as things, and the general unsavoriness of a market in
> body parts. All have some merit. From a legal perspective,
> however, there is really only one major argument against
> permitting a competent adult to sell his or her nonvital organs:
> selling is an act of such desperation that *voluntary* consent is
> impossible.[31]

Another argument based on consent rejects a claim of totality
over the person by the state. William F. May argues that if the
state is allowed total control over the disposition of cadavers, then
that can help reinforce similar claims over the individual while
still living. Establishing a policy of voluntary choice for organ
donation "helps establish the principle of a remainder above and
beyond the claims of the family and state. It establishes the principle of extra-territorality."[32]

Thus one critical issue is whether or not the selling of an organ
will be coerced or chosen. The proverbial "offer that one can't
refuse" is precisely a coerced choice, one that one would not otherwise make. If the price were set high enough, if an individual
were desperate enough, and if personal liberty were neither valued nor protected enough, such transactions would not be voluntary transactions. Also, following May's line of reasoning, a
voluntary system might provide an important defense against
the subtle expansion of state power and the control of the state
over an individual, whether living or dead.

The other major argument against selling organs is the effect such selling could have on altruism and the consequences of that for society. As noted above, the British belief is that organ donations should be altruistic. At present, the American system is based on altruism, although the organ shortage is generating other responses, such as the required request program of New York. Both Paul Ramsey and William F. May argue for altruism because of its beneficial effects on the community. Ramsey says:

> A society will be a better human community in which giving and receiving is the rule, not taking for the sake of the good to come. The civilizing task of mankind is the fostering, the achievement, or the shoring up of the consensual community in general. . . . The routine taking of organs would deprive individuals of the exercise of the virtue of generosity.[33]

May argues that, while not all will share the Christian ideal of "self-donative service by expending [one's self] for the neighbor,"[34] nonetheless society could benefit from the church's institutional support of altruism in society.

Another set of arguments against selling comes from difficuties in using a market system for allocating the organs. First, the market would select only those recipients who can afford to pay. Second, anticompetitive conditions may develop and inhibit the development of a competitive market. Third, the recipient's physician has no incentive to find the lowest priced organ. Finally, because the demand of the recipient is inelastic—he or she has no choices—this my cause prices to rise far above actual costs.[35] Such market difficulties suggest further reasons why organs should not be sold.

The arguments for altruism are both noble and practical. Altruism is better than selfishness; the state should not have total control over one's self; voluntary consent is the precondition for any treatment and a market system may compromise that; the market may not provide a just system of allocation. Yet we are faced with the problem of a shortage of organs. However, as we saw with the case of blood and blood products, the problem of shortage was not completely solved by resorting to commercialization. In fact, the situation appears to be worse with the commercialization of blood than without it, although this may be limited to a particular historical period. Perhaps similar issues would arise with the selling of organs. For the time being, altruism remains the basis for obtaining organs. The selling of organs is seen as coercive and destructive of altruism.

COMPENSATION FOR PARTICIPATION IN RESEARCH

If there is one truism that has been established within the last two decades in biomedical ethics, it is that *the* moral presupposition for ethical research is that the subject's permission must be informed and voluntary. This ethical canon is enshrined in federal regulations and almost every article on the ethics of research. The Institutional Review Board is the main means of ensuring conformity to this norm by reviewing protocols, ensuring their conformity to institutional and federal standards, and monitoring the research to ensure that its requirements are being carried out.

Yet there is a problem that is proving difficult to resolve: Should research subjects be compensated and, if so, how much? Clearly there is a practice of paying research subjects. These payments typically cover items such as reimbursement for transportation costs, lab tests, physical exams, and other medical care. Frequently they involve cash payments to compensate the subject for costs associated with the research, as well as for the inconvenience and exposure to risk that they have undertaken as part of the research.

Almost all agree that the financial cost of research should not be born by the subject. Thus the subject should not pay for extra tests, additional examinations, or the costs of hospitalization or medications while undergoing the research. Finally, if the subject needs to come in for additional visits, these transportation costs would be born by the researchers.

But there is no such agreement about providing a cash payment for participating in research. Such payments are typically made when the subjects are "normals," subjects who are not ill. Whether these individuals are serving as a control group or are testing the effects of a drug or procedure in its first human application, this group of subjects is frequently paid in cash for the commitment of time and exposure to risk. The ethical problem is whether such payments constitute an undue inducement to participate. Can cash payments compromise the voluntariness of consent?

How Much Is Too Much?

The first problem is that there is no fixed sum of money that can be set as a standard of undue coercion. This is so for two reasons. Money has a diminishing marginal utility. Simply stated, this means that typically a dollar means more for the poor person than it does for the rich person. But, second, even within similar income groupings, some individuals attach more value to money than others of the same group do. Thus considerations of quality of life may cause one person to change occupations and locations almost annually while others remain in the same locality and occupation all their lives.

An additional problem is that the value of money must be weighed against the willingness of individuals to accept risks. Some may refuse a large monetary offer, even though money has a high value for them, because they are unwilling to accept high risks. Others, who value money less, may nevertheless put themselves at considerable risk to gain additional money, because they are not uncomfortable with risks.[36]

While recognizing that the dividing line is thin, three factors can be used to help evaluate whether or not an inducement is undue. First is the recognition that individual freedom is not the only or, necessarily, the highest value. While permitting an opening for paternalism, affirming the importance of other values, such as respect for persons or concern for the vulnerable, helps ensure that subjects are more adequately protected. Second, one must consider the nature of the risk. Is one being exposed to a disease which has a high degree of morbidity; is one consenting to another test's being run while in the process of having a major work-up; is the risk of driving to the research site higher than that of participating in the research itself; does the procedure have a mortality risk associated with it, such as undergoing cardiac catheterization? What is difficult to determine is whether the compensation is offered to compensate the subject for his or her time, effort, and exposure to risk or whether the only way to obtain subjects is to present them with the infamous "offer they can't refuse." Third, and perhaps most helpfully, "Inducements are undue if they prompt subjects to lie, deceive, or conceal information that, if known, would disqualify them as participants in a research project."[37] The point here is that the subject knows or discovers that he or she is not qualified—perhaps by reason of pregnancy, age, or the required use of other medications—but conceals this information because the price is right. The compensation is undue because it causes unethical behavior in the potential subject and because it may invalidate the findings of the research.

There is a social and ethical expectation that subjects be fairly compensated for their time and the exposure to risk to which they submit themselves. But it is equally clear that such compensation cannot compromise the quality of the consent. When such is the case, the consent may be neither voluntary nor informed. Obtaining subjects under such circumstances would violate their rights and constitute unethical research.

Selling One's Body

A second major issue concerns selling the disposition over the use of one's body or body parts. The ethical issue is "whether and under what conditions there are aspects of one's own person that are alienable."[38] If one considers the person and the body to be coextensive or if one affirms that the body cannot be totally or ultimately objectified as philosophers such as Marcel and Merleau-Ponty have, then the question of disposition becomes critical. For to so objectify the body is to destroy the person. But also, if the body or body parts are alienable and can, for example, be sold or rented, then we understand the body and/or its parts to be property and a Marxist analysis is helpful in illuminating critical moral issues.

Marx Wartofsky proposes two models by which to consider research. First is the wage labor model. After arguing that what is at issue is the capacity to put oneself at risk with respect to effects on one's health, Wartofsky argues that this question becomes ethical in the following circumstances, based on analogies from the wage labor model.

(1) Is the person freely and rationally undertaking the risk? (Informed consent, no coercion, etc.)

(2) Is the risk such that the calculable effects amount to an alienation of the person as a whole? In which case, since the person's life and liberty are *un*alienable, this amounts to the sale of an unalienable right, and is ethically objectionable.

(3) Is the researcher competently judging (and is the review board competently evaluating) prospective risks and benefits? And is the principle of protection of the individual subject against unnecessary risk being adequately exercised? . . .

(4) Since the relation of the paid research subject to researcher is one of contract, are the conditions of (1)–(3), as ethical considerations, explicitly formulated in terms of legal requirements on the contract so that it presupposes and embodies them?[39]

The major issue here is that if there is an analogy between selling one's labor and selling one's capacity to undergo risk, they need to be evaluated from the same ethical perspective. This perspective is the contract and the four points made above specify how to evaluate some aspects of that contract. The ethical breakpoint is the alienation of life and liberty through accepting too high a risk which then violates the person by alienating and selling precisely those qualities which help constitute personhood: life and liberty.

The second model which Wartofsky uses to illuminate the ethical dimensions of accepting money to undertake risks in research is prostitution.

I want to suggest that this model is revealing for a particular reason: that here, just as in participation in experimentation for money, what is being bought and sold is something which is taken to be so intimate to one's person, that there is something disturbing in the notion that it is alienable, as a commodity.[40]

At issue here is not the obvious fact that that sexual relations without payment may also be devoid of the qualities that we assume they express but that in prostitution the financial exchange highlights and emphasizes prostitution as an act which degrades human relations because the payment bankrupts the voluntary character needed to make the act human. As Wartofsky notes: "Insofar as the seller alienates the disposition over the use of her body, and the buyer possesses this alienated use, prostitution becomes a paradigm of alienation."[41]

Wartofsky pursues his analogy between prostitution and being paid for research through the following analysis. First, given what we think the ideal sexual relation should be and given prostitution as the alienation of the sexual relation into a commodity-money exchange, the moral objection to prostitution is that it dehumanizes both parties by degrading a profound human relation. Second, the act of human self-sacrifice, such as we have in research, is seen as something essentially human and is ethically praiseworthy. But only when this act is free does it have this noble quality. Thus the two major moral characteristics of the act of self-sacrifice are its intimacy to the person, expressing the essence of the person, and its voluntariness. Third, Wartofsky concludes:

> It is clear where such an argument is heading: the researcher and the paid research subject, in reducing an essential human capacity (to put oneself at risk) to a commodity, are in effect dehumanizing each other! Thus, insofar as the paid research subject participates out of economic need, his act is not free but coerced; and therefore, there is no viable contract in the exchange, but rather a relation of exploitation.[42]

Ethically, then, payment for research is problematic insofar as the subject's freedom to participate in research is constrained or coerced by his or her need for money. This may fatally compromise the possibility of a voluntary consent. Such a situation is not necessarily inherent to research as a scientific enterprise. It is more the function of an economic system "which requires wage labor under the coercion of need."[43] Thus to diminish the possibility of research as exploitative of or alienating to both researcher and subject, one must minimize insofar as possible the coercive nature of the payment or reduce the economic need— a task clearly beyond that of the scientific or academic community.

Summary

Whether or not one fully agrees with either Macklin's or Wartofsky's analysis, one still has to agree that payment of money for participating in research can be coercive and that such coercion can destroy the voluntariness of the consent. With no consent, one is doing it for the money and reducing to a commerical transaction that which is inalienable: one's capacity for self-sacrifice. Participating in research only for the money becomes inherently alienating for both subject and professional because, as Wartofsky says of prostitution, "the seller alienates the disposition over the use of her body, and the buyer possesses this alienated use."[44]

WET NURSES

Understood literally, wet nursing is "the practice whereby a woman suckled another woman's child for pay."[45] More broadly conceived, it refers to a system of infant care, either in the wet nurse's home or in the home of the birth mother. References to the practice are found in second-century Rome, the Renaissance, and in premodern and modern England and France. Plutarch, for example, argued that "the goodwill of foster mothers and nurses is counterfeit and assumed; they love for hire." The practice was also known in America.[46]

Explanations of the Phenomenon

Several general explanations are given for the practice. The first argues, psychoanalytically, that the practice is a form of "institutionalized abandonment"[47] of children. The pattern of having the child spend his or her earliest years with a wet nurse continued up until the eighteenth or nineteenth century, in spite of arguments against the practice. While engaged in primarily by the upper classes or nobility, the middle classes also participated in the practice.

The second explanation, similar to the psychoanalytic explanation, is primarily cultural and relies on Philippe Ariès's construction of the concept of childhood. In the past, adults were indifferent to children because of high infant mortality. Little was invested in them and they were frequently put out to nurse. "Any mother who could afford to hire a wet nurse would never sacrifice her sleep, her social life, her sexual pleasure (intercourse was supposed to interfere with lactation), or her small earnings in the store or shop in order to suckle and care for her own baby."[48] When childhood was discovered and appreciated as a value, cultural and familial patterns changed and mothers began to nurse their own children.

The socioeconomic explanation supports the predominance of wet nursing by arguing that women were now working in urban shops, family-run stores, or mills, and in these circumstances it was impossible for them to nurse their own infants. "Thus, when even poorer peasant women offered to breast-feed and care for the urban women's babies in the country for very modest wages, a bargain was struck."[49] The practice ceased when the participation of women in the nonagricultural work force decreased, when rural incomes rose, and when birth rates decreased and bottles and rubber nipples were developed.

The fourth explanation presents wet nursing as a safe alternative among the limited modes of feeding an infant. If the mother refused or couldn't feed her child because of cultural, socioeconomic, or physical reasons, in the absence of technical means to feed the child, the wet nurse was a reasonable, if not the only, alternative. Once bottles, nipples, and sterilized cow's milk became available, the need for wet nurses declined.

A final explanation suggests that paternal jealousy of the infant in bed with the mother, along with the emotional and temporal demands of nursing, may have been a motivating factor for the practice.[50] The husband may have resented the infant's access to his wife's body that he had been denied because of the pregnancy.

Although perhaps a phenomenon practiced primarily by the upper classes, wet nursing was widespread and continued, as an organized practice, until the early twentieth century, at least in France.

Who Were the Wet Nurses?

We are fortunate in having a record of a fourteenth-century physician's description of the qualities and characteristics of a wet nurse. She should be

> between twenty-five and thirty-five years, as much like the mother as possible, and let her have good color and a strong neck and strong chest and ample flesh, firm and fat rather than lean but by no means too much so, her breath not bad,

her teeth clean. And as for her manners, guard against the proud and wrathful and gloomy, neither fearful, nor foolish, nor coarse. Let her breasts be between soft and hard, big but not excessive in length, the quantity of her milk moderate, and the color white and not green, nor yellow and even less black, the odor good and also the taste, not salty or bitter, but on the sweet side, and uniform throughout, but not foamy, and abundant. And note that the best is one who has her own male child. And beware of the one who "goes bad" such as one whom her husband won't leave alone, and one whom you find gravid.[51]

It is unclear how many wet nurses may have fit that description. Yet many served in this capacity. Edward Shorter argues,

> The wet nurses, drawn from the agricultural laborers, marginal peasants, and unwed mothers (who often got pregnant in order to lactate and thus market themselves) were desperately poor, harried creatures who generally lived in rural hovels.[52]

Several other studies confirm that wet nurses were drawn from the peasant, serf, or lower classes.[53] Frequently the conditions in these rural areas were so desperate that infant mortality was exceptionally high.[54] Nonetheless wet nurses were frequently sought and, in France and Germany, for example, a variety of official and unofficial bureaus existed to match wet nurses with families.[55]

Thus the general impression is that the wet nurse was a poor woman, typically peasant or rural, more often than not taking the infant to her home, and keeping the infant, if he or she survived, for one or several years.

This pattern is broken somewhat in England, but not by the conditions of class and location, for the British wet nurses were poor—though not among the poorest—and lived in rural areas. They did differ in that there was not a similar guild arrangement nor were there associations supported or organized by the church or state to serve as matchmakers. Local parishes did provide wet nurses for the poor and abandoned within their areas. Additionally, foundling hospitals provided this service for orphans and other poor children. In general, in these situations the infant mortality rate was lower and the pay on average higher than on the Continent.[56] The other women who wet-nursed did so as private individuals, frequently with the husband, who would be in the city for other business, as the broker.[57] The wages, as well as the status of the position, appear to be higher than on the Continent. Infant mortality also was lower in England, which may be because the women were from a better socioeconomic class.[58]

The Relation Between Wet Nurses and Infants

That there should be some relation between wet nurse and infant seems reasonable, but to demonstrate what that relation was is difficult. Infants, needless to say, could not report their impressions. The majority of the wet nurses were probably illiterate since they were from the rural classes. And since the parents were not on the scene, they could not make observations.

Nonetheless, there was a recognition that such interactions were important. There was a perception, stemming from at least the medieval period, that mother's milk was another form of placental blood which carried character traits with it as well as physical nourishment.

> Not only physical traits—including the dreaded syphilis—but also characteristics of temperament such as sloth, promiscuity, impiety, could be transferred pre-natally or from nurse to child. In a discourse giving advice on raising Louis XIV, selection of a nurse was to take into account "beauties of the soul . . . so that the prince receives impressions of good habits with the milk . . . and of goodness and wisdom."[59]

There is a rather sharp split on how wet nurses related to the infants entrusted to their care. The difference may reflect class distinctions and whether the nurse was in the home or had the child at her home. And even though care of the child is advertised in medieval Italian carnival songs, actual care is documentable only indirectly.[60] In either event the evidence is scanty.

The memoir literature reveals several instances of fond memories of the wet nurse, who frequently shared in the esteem of the biological mother or, as in the following case, replaced her.

I show more affection and gratitude to the one to whom I owe the most. When the time for your lying-in came you rid yourself of me as of a burden that was inconvenient . . . while instead my nurse continually caressed me, nourished me for two years with her own milk and by her care and trouble brought me to the vigorous manhood in which you see me at present.[61]

This attitude is present in a Russian experience also.

My wet nurse at first seems quite mysterious, almost indistinguishable. I recall myself lying, at night, not in a cot, not in my mother's arms, and invariably crying. Sobbing and wimpering, I kept repeating the same word over and over again, calling somebody, and then somebody did appear in the gloom of the poorly lit room, took me in her arms, and lay me to her bosom—and all was well. . . . My wet nurse, who was passionately devoted to me, does appear a number of times after this in my memories, sometimes in the distance, stealing a look at me from behind some other people, sometimes kissing my hands and face and weeping over me.[62]

And from sixteenth-century England we have the following testimony.

You bore me but nine months in your womb, but my nurse kept me with her teats the space of two years; that which I hold of you is my body, which you gave me scarce honestly, but that which I have of her proceedeth of her affection. And moreover as soon as I was born, you deprived me of your company, and banished me from your presence; but she graciously received me . . . between her arms and used me so well, that she has brought me to this you see.[63]

In spite of these glowing testimonials about the successes of wet nursing, there is another side: trauma or physical harm. Ross, for example, argues that wet nursing caused a double displacement: immediately postbirth, from the mother to the wet nurse, and postweaning, from the wet nurse to the mother and the rest of the family.[64] While the first displacement may not have necessarily been problematic, one can understand the possibility of traumatic separation from the wet nurse, after a period of perhaps two years, and reintegration in an established family.

Shorter, however, argues that wet nursing—as a practice—was harmful:

> traditional nurses as a rule were indifferent beyond belief to the welfare of the babies they took in. Children were commodities for them, just as, let us say, cocoa futures are commodities for the modern trader. And they acted invariably to maximize their profits, as a trader would with any standardized interchangeable unit in the marketplace. For the commodities dealer, one sack of cocoa is not intrinsically more marvelous or precious than any other given sack. So also for the mercenary nurses of the eighteenth century.[65]

Shorter indicates that at one foundling hospital, 60 percent of the infants had their wet nurse changed at least once. Also there was an exceptionally high infant mortality rate among infants cared for by wet nurses.[66] Whether this was caused by the harsh conditions of rural life or by indifference of the nurse is unclear, on a case by case basis. Shorter strongly argues that the commercialization of the practice—with all of its market incentives— was the cause of infant mortality and of the lack of a caring relation between wet nurse and child.

> After having raised a baby for seven years in your home, would you then give it up? Yes, you would, because the hospital paid higher rates for newborn than for older children. Attached though you may be to Cocoa Lot 688, you unload it at the first opportunity if the price drops. And no money at all? No infant care. In the department of the Eure, where unsettled conditions had delayed fee payments during the Revolution, nurses simply stopped coming, and those infants abandoned at the hospitals perished there.[67]

Sussman's study also indicates similar infant mortality and similar difficulties between infants and families when the wet nurses were not paid.

Thus there are two sharply differing perspectives on the impact of the wet nurse on the infant. Again, data are limited, but it is clear that on the Continent there was a high infant mortality rate. Whether this was due primarily to neglect because of non-payment or because of the harshness of life and its effect on infant mortality, is unclear. Obviously the commercial motive was present and obviously some nurses established significant relations with their charges. The absence of some of these situations in Britain may help explain the lower infant mortality there as well as the higher esteem in which the wet nurses were held.

DISCUSSION

Several issues have been raised with respect to the commercial disposition of body parts. First among these is the impact of such practices on altruism. In England, altruism remains strong enough to ensure ample blood supplies. In the United States, the picture is a bit more complex since Titmuss did his study. For example, though a market system was originally in place, presently about 70 percent of all whole blood is now donated. Paid donors constitute about 3 to 4 percent of all donors.[68] Thus altruism is operative in the United States, although problems of coordination and competence in developing institutions to collect blood seem to help explain why many turned to the market to obtain blood.

With respect to obtaining organs, altruism has not worked in the United States and efforts are being made to use an "opt out" or "required request" system; in England, altruism remains in place, with attempts to replace it with an "opt out" system being rejected.

Whether the relative homogeneity of the British culture facilitates altruism or not is unclear. But typically England has enjoyed a remarkable cultural unity and a sense of "all being in it together" which has, no doubt, helped maintain the strong bonds that makes altruism more feasible. Thus blood supplies remain adequate.

Such homogeneity does not exist in the United States as a culture, though clearly it does exist among groups within the population. Can the market mechanism serve as a type of substitute for altruism to ensure adequate blood supplies and, perhaps, organs? With respect to blood, the market hasn't worked. Blood supplies are typically inadequate and there is waste and high overhead costs. Would the situation be any different with organs? If the blood model is an appropriate analogy, the answer will be no. But since some may wish to sell their organs after death, with payment going to heirs or into a trust fund, for example, then some may be motivated to do so.

Additionally, one must consider the effects of the market on the process of allocation. Such a market will be a sellers' market because those who need organs frequently have few alternatives other than a transplant. This is particularly so with the heart in the light of the difficulties with the artificial heart. In this market, the ability to pay may become the only criterion for procurement of organs, with many of those most in need of an organ excluded. This may have profound social effects with respect to how the poor or middle class—already in a precarious situation with respect to health care—perceive themselves and their position within society.

Two other market issues are important. First, there are no disincentives to obtaining a less expensive organ. Since payment is private and since the physician's task is to obtain one, the only limit is the ability to pay. Thus there is a strong incentive for prices to rise. Second, the quality of the organ may be compromised. If the sale of the organ occurs *after* death, the seller may have no incentive to maintain a healthy lifestyle. One could envision mandating annual checkups or a contract prohibiting certain behaviors, but enforcement would be difficult. Thus while an individual may have purchased an organ, the market cannot guarantee the quality of that organ at the time of the transplantation.

Coercion is another important issue. Clearly some inducements are undue and totally undercut individual liberty. The condition of some people is so desperate that they will do literally anything to solve their problem—even if such a solution may not be in their best interest. Concerns about liberty, human dignity, and altruism argue against a system of letting some make offers others can't refuse. But defining such an offer is exceptionally difficult, given differing perceptions about the value of money and the acceptability of various risks. Presently, the policy is to permit no offers. But since organs are in short supply and altruism appears not to be an adequate motivator, other strategies—which still are not market strategies—are being proposed. Perhaps such encouraged altruism that comes from an "opt out" or "required request" system may increase the supply. There still appears to be a reluctance to go to a total market system.

Finally, there is the issue of alienation coming from the selling of a body part, whether through selling blood, being paid to undergo research, or being a wet nurse. The critical issue is whether such selling violates one's personhood by selling that which is inalienable: one's life or liberty. When these essential qualities of personhood are compromised, then one's body becomes a commodity and one is alienated. That such commodification of the body can happen is clear. That it does in all cases is unclear. But there is an ethical danger here of viewing the body—and ultimately the person—as yet another commodity that can be packaged and marketed. Such reduction of the person and the body to an object is destructive of personhood. Such a practice could remove the last remaining restraints to viewing the person as totally at the service and disposal of the state. Allowing or encouraging the selling of the body or body parts may compromise human freedom and in so doing ensure the destruction of the person through his or her commodification.

·3·

Background Moral Issues

An Overview of the Family

Parenthood has traditionally existed within the context of the family. But while the family has long existed within human society, its precise origins and original forms are lost in the past, and it has presented itself in a variety of forms during its history.

The three major forms of the family are typically described as a multiple family household or extended family, a stem family, and the basic conjugal, or nuclear, family.[1] The multiple family household is extended in two directions. Vertically, it contains the grandparents and grandchildren. Laterally, this family grouping contains the siblings of either (or both) the husband or wife. The stem family contains the mother, the father, the children, and at least one set of grandparents. The basic conjugal, or nuclear, family has no other kin living with it. The mother, father, and children live as a unit unto themselves.[2]

The function of the unit is the basis for its existence. For example, survival almost dictated that individuals band together in some type of extended social unit. If each were left to himself or herself, survival and reproduction would have been impossible. Also such units provided a means to transfer property and to ensure the survival of one's lineage. Since the family was, in its early stages, a unit of production, such large, multigenerational groupings were extremely advantageous for survival.

The shift from a rural to urban culture helped facilitate the development of the stem family. One the one hand, less space

36

was available in urban contexts and, on the other, fewer individuals were needed to produce goods. Also a division of labor occurred in that the children were apprenticed out to other craftspersons to learn a trade. While the family carried out the role of orderly transfer of property and provided a guarantee of immortality through the survival of the lineage, its form changed with the times.

The transition to the modern family—our nuclear family—was facilitated by what Edward Shorter calls domesticity:

> the family's awareness of itself as a precious emotional unit that must be protected with privacy and isolated from outside interests.[3]

This sense of domesticity had three major impacts on the traditional family of the last century. First, romantic love replaced material considerations in the seeking of a spouse. Concerns of property and the uniting of families for political or financial gain gave way to the selection of spouses on the basis of the mutual affection they had for each other. In short, arranged marriages were replaced by the reality of courtship. Second, mother-child relations were emphasized. Children were recognized as intrinsically valuable, and mothers began to put the interests of the child first. Thus the concept of childhood came into existence. Families made an emotional investment in the child and the home became a center of emotional warmth within which the family could locate itself. Third, domesticity itself began to seal off the family from the larger community. The traditional family—in either the extended or stem version—was open to the community and its life was lived rather publicly. The contemporary family presents a zone of privacy, a barrier between the world and the members of the family. What constitutes the modern family is its self-awareness as a voluntary grouping based on mutual affection between partners and extending to offspring, while existing as an autonomous unit within a larger social system.[4]

Such a family is no longer the basic unit of society. The nuclear family is a unit of consumption rather than a unit of production. Because of this major shift, it is no longer the exclusive, and perhaps not even the primary, means of the socialization of children. Functions, such as education, job training, and religious formation, are performed outside the home by experts. The family exists unto itself, unconnected as a unit to society and functioning as a haven from an impersonal world.

As one could surmise, this is asking a lot of any institution, and it comes as no surprise that the nuclear family is in transition. Shorter identifies two reasons for this. First, there is an inherent instability in the couple because it is not supported by any other social institutions. The relation is based on romantic love and separated from society and exists for the sake of itself. When the affection fades or obstacles interfere with the original affection, there is little inherently to hold the couple together. Second, parents experience diminished control over their children. The peer group is the major formative influence for them, continuing the trend of socialization of the offspring outside the family unit. Thus the bonds of mutual affectivity between parents and children may be absent, which in turn makes the dissolution of the family and marriage easier.[5]

Thus we are now in another stage of the development of marriage. Single-parent families are much more common as a consequence of the high divorce rate. And new families, blended because of parental remarriage, are common. Also individuals are living together and having children, while others have children without living together. And homosexuals and lesbians are participating in parenthood, through adoption, by maintaining custody of children from previous marriages, or by using artificial insemination.[6]

Parenting

As forms of the family continue to change, so do individuals' motives to have children. Improvements in prenatal care, the eradication of diseases such as smallpox, and improved sanitation and nutrition have led to a decrease in infant mortality. Thus one needs fewer pregnancies to achieve the desired number of children. Factors such as increased costs of child rearing and an emphasis on quality of life influence the number of children a couple will have. Finally, the broader population pattern of a particular nation can qualify, either directly or indirectly, the number of children a couple will have. Directly, a couple can help a nation achieve its population goals by limiting its family size. Indirectly, a government can use negative or positive inducements to help individuals limit family size.

The motivations for childbearing

Regardless of such policies and practices, parenting and the desire for children are still major concerns for many people. Why is this? Are such decisions personal, social, or some combination of these? One can assume that "Persons decide to have children in the context of an existing childrearing practice and plan their lives in the expectation of the rewards that this practice enables them to enjoy."[7] Thus, while conceiving a child is a personal decision, that decision is made within a social context.

The following summarizes typical motivations for having children.

> Some people have children out of political considerations, to promote the goals of a larger community than the reproductive unit itself (this is an important motivation for having children in Plato's Republic). Some want children for economic reasons. . . . In some societies, people want children for what might be called familial reasons: to extend the family line or family name, to propogate ancestors, or to enable the proper functioning of religious rituals involving the family. Then, too, having children gives parents power over them, in many cases the most effective power they will ever have the opportunity to exercise on an individual basis. Men and women may also look upon parenthood as providing them with the opportunity to demonstrate competence in social roles. Further, persons have children in order to achieve a kind of personal immortality, or because parenthood is considered a part of life, of personal growth, that cannot be experienced in any other way, and hence as an indispensable element of the full life. Finally, persons want children for the altruistic pleasure of having them, caring for them.[8]

Additionally, the Roman philosopher Seneca identified respect for the laws of the country and praise from one's own parents as motivations for having children, in addition to the perpetuation of the family and the enjoyment of the blessings of love.

Augustine, the Christian theologian who was to have a major influence on his tradition, saw parenthood benefiting the individuals by offering them a means of salvation from sexuality. "Marriage provides an honorable and regulated outlet for concupiscence by confining it to the production of children."[9] Arguing against the Manichee philosophy, Augustine argued that only the natural end of intercourse, children, could justify sexual experiences. Thus parenthood was, for Augustine, located within marriage, but each act of intercourse had to be open to conception since parenthood is the justification for intercourse.

Other motives for parenthood are shown in various social science studies. One such study identified over a dozen motivators.[10] First are innate factors suggesting that the various tactile experiences of having a baby are intrinsically rewarding. The problem, a traditional one, is determining whether such factors are genuinely innate or whether they are learned. As the author notes, if there are such innate factors, they are so overlaid by culture that it is impossible to identify them. Psychoanalytic motives are second. These include competition with one's parents, penis envy, and prceiving children as an extension of the self. The third motivation is conformity to social norms. While the specific nature of the effect of social expectations is difficult to measure, parents seem to be influenced by society, specifically regarding family size. Fourth, people identify liking children as another motivator. This refers to the intrinsic liking of children, as well as to an expression of wanting to be generous by helping others and an expression of dependency needs by having someone to care for. Financial gain is a traditional motivator for children, particularly in rural societies and countries without some form of social security. Additionally, families may benefit from tax exemptions and various other benefits such as maternal and paternal work leaves. While these latter forms may not be explicit motivators for having children, they may enter into one's decision making.

Sixth, rearing children historically has provided a role for women. There is, of course, significant debate over whether motherhood should be *the* role for women or simply an option. Nonetheless, for many motherhood is the role and no other options exist. Such perceptions may be class related and serve as a primary means of securing an identity for the individual. Seventh, the marital relation may influence the desire to have children. Some see children as the expression or extension of the mutual love of the couple and others see a child as a way to resolve problems in the marriage, for example, to prevent a marriage from breaking up, to keep the woman in the expected role, or to help the woman meet dependency needs of her own.[11]

Already existing children can also be a motivator. Parents may want their child to have a sibling, may feel that an only child will be unhappy, think that larger families are happier, or may experience pressure from the children to have another brother or sister. The desire for a child of a particular gender presents the ninth motivation. Most couples want a child of each sex, but there is a higher preference for a male child. Thus a couple may have a larger family to ensure the presence of a male.

One's family of origin can provide another source of motivation for children. A couple may be pressured by their parents into having children or they may wish to replicate their own happy home experience.

Religion is an eleventh factor because it can have ethical positions concerning a particular family size and the means to achieve it. Additionally a religion may reinforce traditional roles of women. Other religions may project an ideal family size, may encourage large families to keep up membership in the religion, or keep members from secular activities by having them involved in a large family. And many religions encourage couples to understand children as the special blessings of the divine power.

The desire for pregnancy itself is a twelfth motive for having children. Some women feel better physically and psychologically while pregnant. Others enjoy the special attention given them while pregnant. Pregnancy can also improve the relations between husband and wife, for the husband may be more attentive and tender to his wife while she is pregnant. Sexual relations may improve because the couple need no longer worry about becoming pregnant. And pregnancy can heighten a woman's consciousness of her self as a woman and give her a heightened sense of femininity.

Finally, some other general motives are operative. Parents, for example, may want to live their lives over through their children. Or, children may be seen as another experience that helps one participate in the whole of life. Mothering a child may help a woman who is experiencing role confusion clarify her self-image. Children may also bring relief to an otherwise boring or uneventful life, and children may bring relief from feelings of rejection by the larger society. A family provides a place to be and a way of keeping busy so that feelings of rejection can be displaced.

Additionally, parenthood is an opportunity for individuals who experience various forms of social, economic, and political deprivation to prove themselves or to be somebody in a context that denies them other avenues for such self-definition or self-experience.[12] Even more significantly,

> parenthood is a *precondition* for women's and men's adult roles; i.e., the primary basis for achieving full social participation. Deviations from the established role expectations (e.g. homosexuality, childlessness, single status, etc.) are punished by a variety of social, economic and psychological sanctions.[13]

Thus parenthood is the key which unlocks the gate to other social roles and participation in the life of the society. While one can obviously participate in society without children, being a parent facilitates such participation and helps establish one's place within the broader society. Thus parenthood is universally prescribed and there are few, if any, "socially rewarded alternatives to the performance of parental roles."[14]

This orientation, identified as pronatalism, is particularly important because it defines an almost unconscious cultural bias toward traditional sex roles and implicitly constrains people's options without their even being aware of it. Thus, while pronatalism suggests a probirth orientation and one that encourages reproduction, a significant element in it is "the age old idea that a woman's role must involve maternity—that woman's destiny and fulfillment are closely wedded to the *natal,* or birth experience."[15] This is then wedded to a variety of values and cultural institutions that serve to reinforce traditional roles: nostalgia for a world that was, the social esteem of the family, premarital rituals that both signal and reinforce the expectation that one marry, defining "good" men and women by reference to their participation in family life, and a desire for social stability.[16] Thus discussions of parenthood must take into account that

> reproductive behavior is under stringent institutional control and that this control constitutes, in many respects, a coercive pronatalist policy. Hence, an effective anti-natalist policy will not necessarily involve an increase in coercion or a reduction in the "voluntary" element in reproduction, because individuals are under pronatalist constraints right now. People make their "voluntary" reproductive choices in an institutional context that severely constrains them not to choose non-marriage, not to choose childlessness, not to choose only one child, and even not to limit themselves solely to two children.[17]

Thus we accept parenthood through traditional socialization processes and by having few other role alternatives. This orientation does not deny the value or significance of parenthood but puts it in a different perspective. One the one hand, perhaps we "desire" parenthood not because of choice, but because of our socialization process. On the other hand, some individuals experience so much pressure to become parents because, in addition to their own desires, they have the weight of society on them.

Not being a parent—whether voluntarily or involuntarily—is, therefore, very difficult, for one is running counter to society, to one's sex role, and to the dominant patterns of socialization. Thus the pressures which drive individuals to seek parenthood can be more easily understood.

The nature of parenthood

The motivations for parenthood are many and the incentives significant. Yet in what does parenthood consist? This issue is important for it sets a context for understanding the "norm" of parenthood, as well as helping us understand and evaluate exceptions to this.

The typical distinction is between a social parent and a biological parent. The biological parent is the parent who physically conceives, carries, and gives birth to the child. The social parent is one who raises the child. The social understanding of parenthood leaves open the issue of biology:

> A parent in this sense is any adult who has a continuing obligation to direct some important aspect (or aspects) of a child's development, and a child can have several such parents, including those who actually produced the child, relatives, tutors, day-care workers, and school teachers.[18]

Social parenthood emphasizes the significance of the emotional relation and commitment to children that can stand independent of biological processes. But, while neither denying or deprecating adoptive parents, does this understanding of parenting depart uncritically from biology and sexuality? Is there a connection between biology and parenthood that is morally significant?

One orientation suggests that the nature of parenthood is the desire to produce children:

> The motive, or the end, of parenthood is surely the creation of a whole person, and this takes within its grasp both the begetting and the raising of the child.[19]

The unique dimension of parenthood is the aim of shaping a person in the parent's own image. This includes both the desire to generate the child from the parents' own bodies and to form the child. The parents intend for more of themselves than their values to be in their children. This biological or genetic relation is important for two reasons.

> On the one hand it forms an important part of the characterization of parenthood under which it is desired and, therefore, under which it has special value in human life. On the other hand, it has an important place in the distinctive relation that exists between parents and their children.[20]

This distinctive relation between parents and children is because the biological parents produced or created the children. The commitment to children is not exclusively emotional or a commitment of the will, though surely it is that too. But an emotional commitment and a commitment of the will have "an inherent vulnerability."[21] For "in their thoughts if not in their deeds, adoptive parents could turn to returning or replacing the child."[22] With biological parents this is not an option, for the child is theirs, born from their bodies.

> It is rather that, built around the physical relation, is a framework of thought within which natural parents are conceived of as having a positive creative role which sees the begetting and rearing of children as parts of a single process. And it is through this framework that the distinctive parental bond with the child and acceptance of it, for better or worse, is to be understood.[23]

Thus in this orientation the connection between parenthood and generation is what gives parenthood its special value. Biological parenthood serves as the model for adoptive parents and is what provides patterns and attitudes for others who are not biological parents to follow. Thus adoption is an exception to the norm—but not to be rejected on that account.

> The two parts—begetting and rearing—are clearly complementary to each other and neither is entirely intelligible, as a form of human activity, without the other. Taken together they form a whole, *parenthood*, which is immediately intelligible as something to be desired for its own sake, as something having a place in human values and as something to be protected by a system of parental rights.[24]

Another approach to parenthood also bases its understanding on an analysis of sexual intercourse and the nature of the male-female relation. This approach begins by distinguishing "making" from "begetting."

> A being who is the "maker" of any other being is alienated from that which he has made, transcending it by his will and acting as the law of its being. To speak of "begetting" is to speak of quite another possibility than this: the possibility that one may form another being who will share one's own nature, and with whom one will enjoy a fellowship based on radical equality.[25]

Begetting establishes a link in intercourse between the procreative and relational goods of marriage. Each strengthens the
other and each is threatened by the loss of the other. For the
relationship is "protected from debasement and loss of mutuality
by the fact that it is fruitful."[26] And the true nature of procreation
is "secured by its belonging to the man-woman relationship."[27]
What is important in this perspective is not to examine each and
every act of intercourse within marriage as an isolated phenomenon but rather to recognize:

> As a whole, then, the married love of any couple should (bar-
> ring serious reasons to the contrary) be both relation-building
> and procreative; the two ends of marriage are held together
> in the life of sexual partnership which the couple live to-
> gether.[28]

Within this perspective, parenthood is an essential part of the
marital relation; while individuals can obviously procreate outside
of marriage, whether biologically or artificially, such acts violate
the structure of the relation because they do not serve to enhance
the relation, nor does the procreation necessarily grow out of
the mutuality of commitment of the partners to each other.

This perspective locates parenthood within the order of nature
as well as in the order of relationships. For to separate these
orders violates our human nature and leads us to self-alienation
because what then issues from nature and relationships models
more an act of production than an act of procreation. To be
most fully itself, parenthood emerges from both natural and relational realities.

But parenthood can also be a matter of choice—unrelated to
one's biology, one's marital status, and one's sexual preference.
One becomes a parent because one chooses to, not because of
the "natural" culmination of a relation.

> I submit humbly but confidently, that using an argument to
> exclude adult people from parenthood which is based solely
> on the definition of an individual's sexual practice, is unten-
> able and uncivilized. Adult people have in their gift the right
> to dispose of their own reproductive potential as they them-
> selves think suitable.[29]

This position assumes that sexual expression is defined and determined by choice, not nature, that the sexual preference of parents has no detrimental effect on the raising of children,[30] and that negative judgments about homosexual or lesbian parents reflect social prejudices.

Thus parenthood is understood as a right to be exercised just as other rights are. The grounding of the right is the autonomy and freedom of the person, not the person's nature or position in a relationship. This perspective coheres well with our culture's acceptance of unconstrained liberty in the private sphere of action. Parenthood can thus be understood as an act of self-exploration or self-disclosure.[31]

This liberal orientation is also reflected in legal analyses which focus on the right to reproduce.[32] John Robertson identifies three interests which ground the right to reproduce: the survival of the species and genetic immortality, the meaning of the transfer of genes to a new generation, and the possibility that women may find childbearing to be important to their sense of identity.[33] Given these interests, as well as the importance of reproduction in an individual's life and the privacy in reproductive decisions based on Supreme Court decisions on contraception and abortion, Robertson argues for a right to procreate and bear a child which will be immune from restriction unless a compelling state interest is at stake.

> Even if the reason one copulates illegally is for the purpose of conceiving, bearing, giving birth to, and parenting a child, the state's interest in regulating sexual morality, preventing illegitimacy, or structuring society through the traditional family will override. In short, requiring marriage for people who want to conceive is constitutional.[34]

However, Robertson also argues that once conception has occurred, then the rights of the unmarried become coextensive with the married. Illegitimacy is not a sufficient state interest to mandate an abortion. Nor can unmarried persons be prevented from parenting, once the child is born, unless they demonstrate that they are unfit and that the child will suffer.[35]

Thus, while there may be an interest in limiting the exercise of the right of procreation to those who are married, the fact of conception puts other rights into play. Even though a couple's situation may not be recognized by the state, in effect their right to reproduce cannot be effectively regulated. Once conception has occurred, the only restraint on the parents is their demonstrated unfitness to raise a child by causing him or her harm. Developing mores in the United States certainly seem to support this view of the right to procreate.

Summary

Defining parenthood is a complex and difficult task. Issues of biology, psychology, anthropology, sexual roles and stereotypes, state interests, religion and philosophy, and views of human nature all come into play. Yet I think O'Donovan is correct in suggesting that the major distinction is between locating parenthood in nature and in freedom. The former view situates parenthood in a web of preexistent relations and structures, while the latter understands parenthood as essentially independent of any constraints of nature and society other than those stipulated by the individuals involved. Seeing parenthood as an act of freedom certainly allows for more possibilites with respect to modes of conception, the sexual preference of the parents, and understanding the children's relation to the parents.

One must also consider how society and the culture influence a couple's motivations to become a parent. Regardless of one's philosophical understanding of parenthood, the culture is extremely critical in defining the significance of parenthood and in impelling people to become parents.

Yet culture and philosophy do not act independently. Understanding parenthood as part of the order of nature certainly grounds many motivations for parenthood and helps define roles for parents. Understanding parenthood as choice has without doubt changed but also enriched our view of conception and the circumstances and conditions under which one becomes a parent. Nonetheless the incentive to become a parent remains strong. Whether this is biological or a consequence of pronatalist socialization is unclear. What is clear is that understanding parenthood and its motivations is a complex business.

COERCION

Is there a sense in which the desire to have children is coercive; is there a corresponding sense in which the utilization of the technologies of reproduction are coercive? These questions could also be considered from the perspective of freedom: Is the choice to have children a free choice; can one freely choose to utilize the technologies of reproduction? Two dimensions need examining: coercion and the desire for children.

Perspectives on Coercion

That individuals and societies exert pressures to act in particular ways is clear. The manner of such influence, however, is quite unclear. The frequently repeated quote from *The Godfather*—"the offer you can't refuse"—highlights our ambivilance about freedom and coercion. On the one hand is an offer; on the other, the offer is construed in such a way that it cannot be refused. Is this coercion, the acceptance of a bribe, a free choice, or simply no choice at all?

Ruth Macklin identifies a conceptual continuum with respect to these questions: coercion, manipulation, seduction or temptation, persuasion, and indoctrination or education.[36] For Macklin, coercion involves two elements: a threat of force or bodily harm against one's self or a relative and doing something one would otherwise not do voluntarily or intentionally. Manipulation involves influencing someone's choice by making generous offers of material goods or higher status. This type of influence is particularly effective when individuals are weak or dependent or are in an institutional context which renders them vulnerable. Seduction or temptation involves the offer of some pleasure or good but in such a way that choice or responsibility is not totally voided. The moral assumption is that a person can avoid giving in to temptation—and is in fact expected to—but may not be able to resist a coercive proposition. Persuasion relies on the use of reason, argument, and entreaty to persuade someone of the wisdom, correctness, or desirability of a particular option. Education involves the development of skills and the providing of role-models. The purpose of education is to help the individual become autonomous or to accept responsibility for her or his position within the society. Indoctrination involves the communication of one mode of action or way of thought as the correct way. This is typically accomplished by controlling the curriculum, by the screening of teachers, and control of information and access to alternative modes of thinking and reasoning.

Michael Bayles presents another perspective on coercion.[37] Bayles begins by making several distinctions. First, coercion may be occurrent or dispositional. Occurrent coercion involves direct application of physical force to cause a particular behavior in another person. For example, one individual forces a knife into the hand of another and holds it there as she inserts it into the back of a third individual. Dispositional coercion—the more common type—occurs when one threatens another with a sanction if the latter fails to act as requested. This type of coercion requires that the victim's behavior be voluntary; it is assumed that the victim would have acted differently had he or she not been threatened with the sanction. Thus the victim of dispositional violence always has a choice, but what choice is made depends on the victim's beliefs about the "comparative importance of not doing what he was told and of the threatened sanction."[38]

Sanctions serve two functions. First, they may simply teach a lesson. Second, sanctions may be imposed until the individual does as she or he is told. If sanctions are applied, however, coercion has failed. For Bayles, the "essence of successful attempts at coercion lies in getting persons to act by means of threats alone without having to impose sanctions."[39] And sanctions are seen to involve deprivations and harms, not rewards or benefits, which there are the consequences of a bribe. This is primarily to help keep clear the distinction between a sanction and a bribe.

Bayles summarizes his position on coercion as follows.

> Coercion is one form of the exercise of power over another. It is distinguished from other forms by X's further intention of harm to Y if Y does not act as X intends. In other forms of the exercise of power over another X either has no further intention or intends a benefit for Y if Y does as X desires. Coercion is the most morally offensive form of the exercise of power over others because the agent intends to affect the

victim's behavior and uses or is willing to use physical force or harm to do so.[40]

Bernard Gert offers another perspective on coercion.[41] I will first summarize his perspective and then amplify it.

> In my view, only someone with the ability to will can act freely or can act under coercion, that is, only voluntary actions are done freely or under coercion. Unreasonable incentives are needed in order to define both of these concepts. A man acts freely if and only if he acts voluntarily and does not do so because of any unreasonable incentives. A man who acts voluntarily, but only because of some unreasonable incentives, does not act freely. If the unreasonable incentives were the result of a threat of evil by someone, then he acted under coercion. If the unreasonable incentives were the result of a promise of good by someone, then he acted under enticement.[42]

First, note the general agreement between Bayles, Macklin, and Gert that goods or rewards are seen as enticements or bribes and are not understood as coercive. Second, Gert distinguishes between the ability to will and freedom. An individual has the ability to will to perform an action "if and only if there are reasonable incentives that would lead him to do that kind of action and reasonable incentives that would lead him not to do it."[43] Thus having the ability to will—acting voluntarily, that is—requires a genuine option of choosing between alternatives. Freedom, on the other hand, involves both acting voluntarily *and* not because of unreasonable incentives. Thus a person could act voluntarily, but not freely—because of unreasonable incentives.

For Gert, then, the issue of coercion revolves not merely around the threat of evil but the "threat of evil which provides an unreasonable incentive."[44] The unreasonable incentive's interference with freedom is what makes it coercive. One may act voluntarily, but not be held morally accountable because one has not acted freely. That is, one is not accountable because one was coerced.

Gert also distinguishes coercion from other forms of persuasion. Enticements differ from coercion because instead of offering unreasonable incentives, they promise some good. "The mere gaining of a good, no matter how great, does not force one to do anything."[45] Reasoning is also another way to try to get someone to do your bidding. Typically, the reasoning party says "that certain good or evils will result from the action of the person reasoned with, without any intentional action by the reasoning party."[46] Negotiation, while including a wide range of maneuvers in its meaning, is not coercive precisely because "neither side is in a position effectively to threaten the other side with unreasonable incentives."[47] Thus there are a range of activities which we may use to have other people act or do our bidding which are not coercive and which, therefore, do not compromise our moral accountability.

Willard Gaylin examines the major limits on coercion, particularly physical coercion: "anything that involves integration and constancy is not coercible on a physical level."[48] Further physical threats are limited by both their threatening power and by how they are perceived. Once the threat is carried out, it has no further power and if someone does not perceive something as threatening, it is not threatening.

The more critical form of coercion is the psychological:

> This coercion would not simply involve forcing a person to do that which you will but rather forcing him through the manipulation of his emotions to *will* that which you will. If you exploit the anxieties of a person rather than his reason, and this may be done with or without his awareness, you are coercing behavior, often without either the recognition or admission of coercion on either part.[49]

Thus coercion can become institutionalized and individuals may be so accustomed to these forms of behavior that they are not experienced or perceived as coercive. The forms of behavior so coerced are perceived as normal behaviors, freely chosen and freely accepted. As Gaylin observes:

> The "black is beautiful" movement recognized the profoundly coercive effect of the majority prototype. The black power movement (and similarly women's liberation) may perforce,

by the urgency of its need and the revolutionary reverses in thinking and feeling patterns it is demanding, fall occasionally into extreme positions which will permit the majority to reject its contentions as unsophisticated. They are not. It was a profound insight to recognize that the majority prototype was the club which has been used to beat the blacks into submission.[50]

Thus in our considerations of childbearing, we need consider not only whether or not there are any sanctions imposed which philosophically would be coercive but also whether or not the process of acculturation may be coercive.

Coercion and Childbearing

As with all other acts, we decide to have children within a context. How we understand that context will be important for determining whether or not the desire for children is coercive.

The first context is psychological. For example, in speaking of the desire to have children, Shulamith Firestone says that "we don't know how much of this is the product of an authentic liking for children, and how much is a displacement of other needs."[51] She identifies these needs as "the attempted extension of ego through one's children—or in the case of the man, the 'immortalizing' of name, property, class, and ethnic identification—and in the case of the woman, motherhood as the justification of her existence."[52] One can consider these as various goods; to the extent that they are, they may not be coercive.

Next, a more cultural orientation is described by Linda Gordon who notes:

Childlessness spells for many people not only loneliness but the threat of economic insecurity in old age; whereas the hope, often subconscious, for immortality through the family reflects not only the desire to pass on property or prestige, but often an emotional need to make a mark as a human being, to feel one's life as significant and lasting. Child raising seems, deceptively, to offer an area in which adults have power to create human value according to their, not their employers', direction. These factors make children potentially the victims of adults' unsatisfactory lives. These pressures systematically push reproductive decisions beyond the reach of technological solutions. Only the liberation of children from the burden of being useful to adults can make childbearing a free choice, emanating from the desire to perpetuate human life, not oneself.[53]

Here a number of incentives show up, some of which have potentially negative consequences on the child or children. Gordon clearly indicates that she thinks these incentives potentially compromise the freedom of reproductive decisions, although they may not be coercive.

Third, one must consider the possibility of a pronatalist bias within the culture. This point, discussed in the previous chapter, suggests that parenthood is the precondition for all other adult roles for men and women and that, while individuals can quite obviously function socially without children, there are, in fact, few socially rewarded alternatives to parenthood.

Judith Blake was the first to identify this "pronatalist bias" that at best encourages or at worst coerces people in deciding whether or not to have children.[54] Essentially, Blake argues that all societies have organized themselves in such a way as to ensure survival by establishing forms of social control, based in institutions, that promote specific forms of behavior.

The mechanisms for such control are the typical ones. Socialization into the mores and roles of society from the beginning of one's life. Social interaction which puts us in contact with norm-enforcing behavior. And, finally, social limitations on acceptable role alternatives available by reinforcing the socially acceptable ones and sanctioning deviant roles. As social functions, childbearing and parenting are under these same sorts of social controls. These involve the individual "in an articulated and coercive set of constraints."[55] And while the individual has choice among fixed alternatives, these choices are influenced by past experiences and the expectations of who he or she is to become. "His behavior is 'voluntary' only in a restricted sense—not in the sense of being unpatterned, uncontrolled, or unrestrained."[56]

The effect of this structuring of social controls is clear.

In effect, regardless of whether a typical birth cohort of individuals contains a large proportion of persons who might be unsuited to family life, human societies are so organized as to attempt to make individuals as suited as possible, to motivate them to want to be suited, and to provide them with little or no alterative to being suited as they mature. By fiction and by fiat, parenthood is the "natural" human condition, and to live one's life as a family member is the desideratum. In this context individuals make their reproductive "choices."[57]

Thus Blake sees freedom or reproductive choice as limited by the social constraints in which we find ourselves. And while she recognizes that we take such socialization as both legitimate and necessary,

research suggests that socialization for sex-typed personalities goes well beyond the constraints on individuals required for social order. It actually represents the enforcement of the society's commitment to a specific goal—reproduction.[58]

Martha Grimez, in an admission of honesty rare for anyone, admits that she at first rejected Blake's argument but that she became convinced that Blake was correct by her rereading of the literature in the light of Blake's arguments. Grimez argues that deviation from the pronatalist posture is "punished by a variety of social, economic, and psychological sanctions,"[59] and that "reproductive behavior is under stringent institutional control and that this control constitutes, in many respects, a coercive pronatalist policy,"[60] defined as "the existence of structural and ideological pressures resulting in socially prescribed parenthood as a precondition for all adult roles."[61]

Grimez makes two major observations about pronatalism. First, traditional feminist analysis of the right to reproduction ignored the pronatalist dimensions. She argues this because *"the right of women not to have children was not clearly and specifically incorporated in the feminist analysis and critique of reproduction."*[62] That is, the traditional feminist analysis focused only on two questions: how many children to have and when to have them. The question of *whether or not* to have them was not asked—indeed not even thought of. Consequently, Grimez argues that traditional feminism was supportive of pronatalism because it omitted this important element of critique and contributed to the pressures on women to have children.

Second, Grimez presents an explanation for the universality of the role of parenthood.[63] First, from a functional point of view, universal parenthood was necessary because of high mortality rates. Second, capitalism produced a division of life into public and private spheres, and women were assigned the role of reproducing future workers for the public sphere. Such division has led to the oppression of women.

> Third, sexism and pronatalism are mutually interrelated and support each other by providing compensatory ideologies and practices that relieve the tensions and contradictions they create in the relationships between the sexes and between generations.[64]

Thus, as Grimez observes, the exploitation of male workers is made bearable by male supremacy and its attendant perks. On the other hand, pronatalist ideologies about the family and women are to compensate for women's oppression inside and outside the home. Given these factors, Grimez concludes, "Structurally and psychologically, family formation is not a choice for either men or women."[65]

Andrea Dworkin provides a strong analysis of the coercive nature of childbearing and motherhood based on natural law or biological arguments, acculturation, and male dominance. And, she argues, it is women themselves who enforce male power and sanctions over women.

> Mothers raise daughters to conform to the strictures of the conventional female life as defined by men, whatever the ideological values of the man. Mothers are the immediate enforcers of male will, the guards at the cell door, the flunkies who administer the electric shocks to punish rebellion.[66]

Dworkin does not argue that women do this because they like it—far from it. They do it because this is their attempt to blend into the environment, to escape the attention of the predator. Socializing the next generation into male values is a form of survival: "this sexual, sociological, and spiritual adaptation, which is, in fact, the maiming of all moral capacity, is the primary imperative of survival for women who live under male-supremicist rule."[67]

Women accept this and perpetuate it because society (Dworkin uses the term "political Right" interchangeably with society) offers to restrain male violence by making several offers.[68] First, the Right offers an ordered form of society, biology, and sexual relations which eliminate chaos from one's life. Second, protection of the home and women's place in it is offered. Third, since the world is a dangerous place for women, the Right offers safety by promising that if the woman is obedient, no harm will befall her. Fourth, rules are provided for both women and men. If women follow their rules, they can survive. The Right promises that men, too, will follow their rules. Finally, if a woman fulfills her function of obedience, sexual submission, and childbearing, she will be loved by men. Additionally, men will be responsible for the material and emotional well-being of women.

Such a process of socialization and set of incentives locks women into a set of behaviors, expectations, and functions. Options that men take for granted are not even perceived by women. To go against this requires significant courage. In so doing, women make themselves even more vulnerable to male violence, as well as rejection by other women whose consciousness remains dominated by the male culture.

For Dworkin, the issue is not whether women are coerced into childbearing. The issue is the universal coercion of women by a male-dominated culture. Thus everything a woman chooses or does is coerced becaused she either, on the basis of her socialization, accepts the putative safety of "women's roles" or because she accepts the offer of safety and security as the best deal she can get in a sexist society. Efforts at liberation are resisted because they remove what little safety women have within the status quo.

Right-wing women saw the cynicism of the Left in using abortion to make women sexually available, and they also saw the male Left abandon women who said no. They know that men do not have principles or political agendas not congruent with the sex they want. . . . They know that every woman has to make the best deal she can. They face reality and what they see is that women get fucked whether they want it or not; right-wing women get fucked by fewer men; abortion in the open takes away pregnancy as a social and sexual control over

men. . . . Her deal promises that she has to be fucked only
by him, not by all his buddies too; that he will pay for the
kids; that she can live in his house on his wages; and she smiles
and says she wants to be a mommy and play house.[69]

So much, in Dworkin's view, for women's choices. But while
one might argue that Dworkin's perspective is extreme, her basic
point is correct. Women are socialized within a male-dominated
culture and on the basis of values that favor males. Such socialization by definition compromises one's freedom by effectively
preventing an alternative vision of reality or other choices from
emerging.

Summary

The discussion of coercion and childbearing locates the biological fact of childbearing in an important social context. The
argument of the various authors shows the subtle and unsubtle
ways in which individuals are led into certain choices either by
being pressured into them socially or simply by having no other
choices available. The crucial question is: Are these choices genuinely coerced?

First, one's ideology clearly influences how one responds. From
Dworkin's perspective, all decisions that women make are coerced
because of the patriarchal structuring of society. While women
make the best deal they can, she argues that such deals are neither
in their best interest nor are they made freely. If, for example,
one understands all acts of heterosexual intercourse to be
coerced, it matters little whether one or many are coercing the
woman. Rape is rape. If one has children only to secure certain
benefits otherwise unavailable or to avoid harm, such a decision
is inherently compromised. For Dworkin, in the present society,
all such alternatives are unreasonable and, therefore, coercive.

However, if one sees male-female relations in a different light,
choices are opened up and are understood and experienced as
less coercive. Assumedly, one still makes decisions within a context, but one may have examined that context critically and freed
oneself of the pressures of stereotypes and role expectations.
Such freedom can be correlated with class and education, but its
source does not negate the freedom of such choices.

Second, one has to consider the place and perception of children in this discussion. Historically, children have been experienced as a good. Often that good was functional: they would provide for parents in their old age, they would help on the farm or with the products the family produced, they could secure immortality for the family, or they would provide for the orderly transfer of property. Clearly, decisions about childbearing in this context assumed certain social agenda. Children were also seen as the means by which a society would survive. Thus it is in society's best interest to develop strategies that ensure the reproduction of the species. Again such decisions are made under social pressure but they also involve certain social and familial goods.

But children are also seen as a good in themselves. They are an enfleshment of the love of the couple, an embodiment of their relationship. In this perspective the existence of children is assumed, taken for granted. Their presence is expected and welcomed because they are an essential part of the project of the couple. Obviously, one will experience and decide about children in a particular social context, but one can order these contexts.

Third, to the extent that we live and participate in society each of us is under the influence of institutions and roles within those institutions. As we develop we interact more completely with our society. Our choices and alternatives are shaped by those who have gone before us and the institutions they have left as their heritage. Thus Blake is correct and hardly controversial when she says, as noted above, that our choices are influenced by past social experience and the kind of person we have been shaped to be. Such a perspective coheres well with Gaylin's psychological perspectives. That is, the most subtle coercion is that of which we are unaware, that which forces us to will what others want us to will. Gert's philosophical analysis compliments this view also by arguing that one is free only when there is a choice between the alternatives and no unreasonale incentives to choose one rather than another.

The question, then, is: Does socialization constitute coercion or guarantee only decisions that are coerced? In part, the answer depends on one's concept of freedom. Blake, for example, suggests that free decisions are "unpatterned, uncontrolled, or unrestrained."[70] In this understanding, no decision could be totally uncoerced. If, for a decision genuinely to be free, it is necessary that there be no constraints on one's decision, then one can think of few decisions that are free. We are constantly being influenced by others, customs, roles, or institutions. If freedom necessarily implies unrestrained or uninfluenced decision making, then freedom is an illusion.

If, however, freedom is understood as the capacity to choose between existing or available alternatives, then freedom is a reality. It is a less grand, but perhaps more realistic concept. But it is freedom nonetheless. Thus, as Gert would argue, one can be influenced by incentives but still be acting freely. Such incentives appear as part of the society in which we live; they are attached to roles and customs. They are sanctioned through various institutions in the society. For Gert, an incentive becomes coercive when it is unreasonable, that is, "when it would be unreasonable to expect any rational man in that situation to act on it."[71] The examples of unreasonable incentives that Gert provides are death, severe and prolonged pain, serious disability, and extensive loss of freedom. Thus the fact that one acts on or because of an incentive does not intrinsically mean that one's choice is coerced. The choice can be influenced by an incentive and be free.

Finally, the threat which may be coercive is childlessness. That is, the social consequences of being childless in a pronatalist society may be such that they constitute an unreasonable incentive. This would be the case, for example, if the woman was not able to choose childlessness as well as havng a child. Additionally, being childless can lead to the perception that one is not yet an adult. Also, childlessness frequently precludes one from full participation in other adult roles. The extent to which a particular woman cannot choose childlessness because of these and other harmful consequences is the extent to which a woman can be coerced into enrolling into a fertility program.

What can we say, then, about childlessness and coercion? First, assuming that all acts performed in a social context are coerced acts because institutions shape behavior is too broad a statement. Second, for a woman to be coerced she must be so situated that alternatives are not available to her. That is, childlessness must not be an alternative in the sense that she is incapable of choosing such a situation. Additionally, the consequences of childlessness must be experienced as unreasonable harms or incentives.

Coerced behavior may be difficult to verify. Many may not consider the consequences of childlessness to be unreasonable and may not consider them to be harms. But if one judges the individual case, one can understand how such conditions could be verified. If one would see one's life destroyed by childlessness and its consequences, then that is a harm. If one desired children as an essential part of a particular marriage, then such an absence is a genuine harm to that marriage.

Thus the decision to utilize an artificial technology could be a coerced decision but only in a narrowly defined set of circumstances. Additionally, we need to keep in mind an observation that Gert makes:

> Of course, if one wants to do what one is being coerced to do, then one may not mind being coerced. . . . Loss of freedom often does not bother a person unless he wants to do what he is not free to do.[72]

Thus a woman who has been socially conditioned to have a child but who also wants a child may be coerced or forced into having one, but she may not experience such a choice as coercive. And even if she were convinced that she was being coerced into that particular decision, she may still want to have a child. The inability to have a child or to participate in a birth technology may be the more problematic situation for the woman. The potential for coercion is high, but the conditions for coercion are not necessarily verified in each and every situation.

Surrogacy and Coercion

To what extent, if any, is a woman who comes forward to be a surrogate mother coerced? This question is exceptionally difficult to answer because of the paucity of data available on the motivations of surrogate mothers.

Philip Parker is a psychiatrist who works with attorney Noel Keane in the Detroit surrogate program. While some may argue that his data are compromised because of his direct involvement in the program, nonetheless his may be the only longitudinal data available.

Parker has published two studies on surrogates. The initial report gives findings concerning the first 125 potential surrogates interviewed by him. Representative data include: of the first 125, the average age was 25; of 118 applicants, 56 percent were married, 20 percent divorced, and 24 percent never married. Of the first 50 applicants, 40 percent were unemployed, or receiving some form of financial aid or both. Sixty percent were working or had a working spouse. Of 122 women, 89 percent said they required a fee of a least $5000. The range of family incomes was $6000 to $55,000.[73]

Of more critical interest is Parker's findings on motivation.

> In the sample of 125 women, 44 (35%) either had had a voluntary abortion (26%) or had reliquished a child for adoption (9%). Some women believed these previous losses would help them to control and minimize any depressive feelings they might have in response to relinquishing the baby. A few consciously felt that they were participating in order to deal with unresolved feelings associated with their prior losses. The only applicant who had been adopted had been "forced" at age 14 to relinquish her baby, and she wanted to repeat the experience of relinquishment and master it. One applicant who had had an abortion said that instead of "killing a baby" she wanted to give the gift of a live baby to a loving couple who wanted to have and raise a child.[74]

Parker concludes by identifying several factors that appear to him to have a complimentary relation in determining the decision of whether or not to be a surrogate: "1) the perceived desire and need for money, 2) the perceived degree of enjoyment and desire to be pregnant, and 3) the perception that the advantages of relinquishment outweighed the disadvantages."[75] He also argues that although 89 percent of the women said a fee was a necessary condition of being a surrogate, "it was never a totally sufficient reason for being a surrogate mother, for it was accompanied by varying degrees of factors 2 and 3."[76]

Parker's second published article presents no further analysis of data, but amplifies his discussion of motivation and consent, especially with respect to the role of the psychiatrist in ensuring the voluntariness of the consent.[77] Issues that Parker identifies as important in ensuring the freedom of consent are: freedom from coercion and excessive desire for and susceptibility to financial gain, the relation with the surrogate's spouse, and the desire and need to experience relinquishing a child.[78] These could exert a degree of pressure on the pontential surrogate and compromise her freedom.

Parker also has an unpublished study which follows thirty surrogate mothers through delivery and relinquishment.[79] All the surrogates were white due to parental preference and their average age was 25.3. Twenty-six were married, 3 single, and 1 divorced. Sixteen were Protestant and 14 Catholic. With respect to education, 6 had not graduated from high school, 16 graduated from a high school or had a General Equivalency Diploma and 8 had some college or professional training. There were an average of 2.3 pregnancies and 1.9 previous live births. Seven had had abortions and 3 had given up a child. And 28 of the 30 received a $10,000 fee plus expenses for the pregnancy.[80]

As noted earlier, the motivations for becoming a surrogate clustered around the perceived need for money, the perceived enjoyment of being pregnant, and the evaluation of the advantages and disadvantages of relinquishing a baby. Parker found that all the surrogates who received a fee saw it as a payment for services. Some experienced mild discomfort after receiving the fee, and one refused it after she established a personal relation with the couple.

> In general the fee became less important as the pregnancy developed and as the surrogate established a relationship with the parental couple. After delivery, the fee became unimportant to the surrogate as a motivation for relinquishment.[81]

Additionally, most enjoyed the pregnancy, because of the special attention they received while pregnant, because they were doing something only a woman could do, or because of a sense of accomplishment from doing something worthwhile. Finally, Parker notes that some surrogates used the relinquishment to deal with previously unresolved loss of fetus or child. However, no surrogate has consciously experienced surrogacy only as a means of righting a wrong or as a punishment to expiate guilt. This is especially important in light of the fact that seven of the sample had had abortions, with one having two abortions and another three.

Parker found that loss was dealt with in a variety of ways. Most surrogates saw quickening as a critical experience and from then on began viewing the fetus as the social parents'. Also a relation with the social parents seemed to generate empathy for their situation. Many idealized the social parents and denied any aggressive feelings; others reported sharing in the happiness of the couple. Additionally, a support group for the surrogates was established and this helped establish a sense of belonging and was supportive of the feelings of empathy toward the social parents.

Contact with the social parents was variable. One set of social parents rejected any contact with the surrogate; another had the surrogate visit in their home, went to the physician with her, and was the labor coach. Attachment to the baby by the surrogates was also variable. One fed the baby in a very businesslike fashion and another nursed the baby. Thus the contact ranged from intimate to distant, but no precise data are supplied here with respect to frequency.[82]

Parker found that the surrogates generally expressed transient grief symptoms. Some described feelings of sadness that lasted for weeks. One surrogate experienced crying and sleeplessness for about a month; another experienced these symptoms for about five months (she also lost a close relative during the pregnancy). Many indicated that most of the sadness was because of the loss of the relationship with the couple rather than the loss of the infant. One reported no feelings of loss at all. Some experienced anger and resentment toward the social parents which seemed to occur because the surrogates felt they did not receive enough attention. Some had difficulty expressing this anger to the parents and displaced it to the professionals involved. Three surrogates had therapy to help them deal with their grieving process and one to help her deal with her anger.[83]

The surrogates also expressed concern about how the baby would fare in the future. Many wanted to be updated periodically. Others wanted to maintain a future relation with the social parents. Others were refused such a relation and were angry and unhappy about such exclusion. Interestingly,

Several surrogates consciously expressed a desire to have their own replacement child to help deal with the feelings of sadness and loss. Several are again attempting to be surrogate mothers while a few said they would never do it again. Most surrogates acknowledged increased thoughts of the child on the anniversary of the birth.[84]

Making a determination with respect to the potential coercion of a surrogate is difficult, given the paucity of data. At this time my sense is that the financial gain would be more in the nature of a bribe or inducement, perhaps undue, but not essentially coercive. One may be desperate for money, but not be coerced by its offer. Additionally, as Bayles noted, cash functions as a benefit or reward, not a threat or harm. To say that a cash payment is not coercive, but a bribe, is not to diminish its moral significance. If a bribe is the only way to have someone participate in an action, the legitimacy of that action should be seriously questioned.

With respect to psychological pressures, such as the need to master the sense of loss from an abortion or the giving up of a child for adoption, it is clear that such pressures could be so great as to be coercive, but whether they are is simply unknown. What is critical is to determine if such motivation is common and then evaluate that finding.

Additionally, a woman may be coerced into using a surrogate because of her perception of harm from childlessness or because of the perceived harm to her marriage if she does not participate in the desire of her husband to obtain a child genetically related to him.

ALIENATION

Another issue is the impact of surrogacy on the gestational mother. What, if any, consequences follow from the fact of being artificially inseminated, carrying a pregnancy to term, and then giving the infant to the social parent(s)? The concept of alienation provides a framework for the analysis of this issue.

Perspectives on Alienation

The concept of alienation is one of the major contributions of Karl Marx. While not all aspects of alienation as developed by Marx are relevant to the surrogacy situation, several features of it may shed light on different aspects of it. Although the full theory of alienation needs to be set within an understanding of human nature, a model of society, and a theory of labor, nonetheless several aspects can be highlighted for the purposes of this analysis.

Alienation is a "certain sort of human ill or dysfunction which is especially prevalent in modern society."[85] It occurs when we

> experience our lives as meaningless or ourselves as worthless, or else are capable of sustaining a sense of meaning and self-worth only with the help of illusions about ourselves or our condition.[86]

Seen this way, alienation may be a common experience of all peoples of all cultures. Yet Marx believes that there is something unique about bourgeois and capitalist culture that ensures that such alienation will occur.

Additionally, Marx differs from Hegel and Feuerbach over the cause of alienation. Both of these philosophers see alienation arising from errors or illusions about one's self or place in life. For them, once such illusions are overcome, alienation is removed. The remedy for alienation is a higher stage of self-knowledge or an authentic realization of self.

While Marx agrees that alienation is associated with false consciousness and that religion may be a paradigm of such false consciousness, he does not agree "that alienation *consists* in a condition of false consciousness, or that it is *caused* by one."[87] Rather, "the unhappy consciousness tells the truth in its laments, not in its consolation."[88] That is, for Marx, while illusions are a facet of being alienated, alienation is a real feature of human life. Our lives are alienated because they are meaningless, because the condition of our lives make a fulfilled life impossible. The problem of alienation is the lack of knowledge and power to change one's life. Thus for Marx the struggle is not to reinterpret the world—for a change in consciousness does not eliminate alienation—but to change it. For as long as the capitalistic mode of production and the private ownership of the means of production continue, human potential will be frustrated.

Another way into alienation is through an analysis of various elements in the structure of capitalism and the modes of production. This orientation shows the inner workings of the system and its consequences.

Use value is the value something has to satisfy certain needs. It is an instrumental value specifying to what use something can be put.[89] Exchange value, on the other hand, depends on an entity's becoming a commodity. Something becomes a commodity "when it can be exchanged against the other product."[90] That is, something receives value beyond simple use when it can be exchanged for something else. For Marx, what helps distinguish precapitalistic from capitalistic societies is the exchange of objects on the basis of their use value only. One consumed what one produced and the surplus was exchanged but, since it was on the basis of use, such products did not become commodities. Once transfer occurs on the basis of exchange value, the product becomes a commodity to be bought and sold. This sets in motion a process in which ultimately the objects produced take on a higher value than the workers who produce them. For Marx, this has enormous implications in capitalism:

> everything, which up to now has been considered as inalienable, is sold as objects of exchange, of chaffering. It is the time in which objects, which earlier have been conveyed, but never exchanged, have been given away but never offered for sale, have been acquired but never been bought: virtue, love, conviction, knowledge, consciousness and so on, the time which, in a word, everything has been transformed into a commercial commodity. It is the time of general corruption, of universal bribery or, in the language of economics, it is the time when each object, physical as well as moral, is put on the market as an object of exchange to be taxed at its correct value.[91]

Such transformations of everything into a commodity has social consequences. The individual is reduced from an active participant to an object, subject to the mechanisms of exchange. Second, because of the division of labor, the worker can use only a small part of his or her talents. Thus the worker becomes alien to himself or herself. This division of labor, based on specialization in the light of technical developments in the workplace, has three major consequences: (1) the separation of manual and intellectual aspects of work and a consequent devaluing of the abilities of the worker; (2) the control of work by the capacity of technology; (3) class conflict consequent upon the division of labor.

Essentially then, alienated labor is labor through which the worker creates something that is both detached and taken from him or her by those who do not work but who own the means of production. It is labor that is impersonal, not fulfilling, and keeps the worker in a dependent situation.

Thus, according to Marx, there are three social conditions that give rise to alienated labor: the transformation of the person and his or her labor into a commodity, the division of labor, and private property. These then, as Israel summarizes Marx's thought, give rise to three states of alienation. The worker becomes alien to his or her own activities because they are no longer experienced as a personal need but as an enforced need. The individual is alienated from the results of his or her own activities because the worker does not own the product or reap any of the surplus value, for this is accrued by the owner of the means of production. The worker also becomes alienated from the physical world, the social world, and the human species itself.[92]

Thus alienation reflects the social situation of the worker and his or her place within the society. Alienation is essentially a displacement of the worker from a series of significant relationships in his or her life: self, work, and society. The cause of this, according to Marx, is the private ownership of the means of production which means that the worker has no stake in production, other than that of selling his or her labor. Additionally, even though the object eventually produced is sold at a profit, this surplus value does not go to the worker but stays with the owner. Thus the worker sells his or her labor but does not receive a fair return on that transaction. Consequently, the worker is alienated from himself or herself, from others because they are seen as competitors in the sale of labor, and from society because, by being alienated from self and others, the worker cannot enter into fulfilling human relations.

Commodification or Reification

As noted earlier, an object becomes a commondity when it has exchange value. This means that the object in question has gone beyond its need-satisfaction or use value—what it was designed to do—and now has value because of the possibility of exchanging it for something else or for money. Thus the value of the object is determined not by its intrinsic value or use, but by market value—for what else or how much can it be exchanged.

Two supporting concepts lie behind this idea of commodification. First, each object has a proper or normative function determined in accordance with the intention of the producer. Making an object a commodity breaks or at least deviates from that intention. Second, since the value of this new use is determined by the market, not the intention, it will fluctuate according to supply and demand.[93]

Such commodification also changes the relations between humans by reducing them to means only, not keeping them as ends in their own right. Calculation enters into all aspects of their relations and personal relations are transformed into relations between buyer and seller. This then is accepted as normal or natural and the commodification of objects, persons, and relations no longer appears as something alien.

Humans, too, can have a use value. They can possess and be valued for human characteristics: honesty, love, sympathy, and so on. But they can also have an exchange value. This is the value the person possesses as the acquirer of goods. Additionally, this exchange value would be built on the person's utility with respect to labor power. An object relation would be one characterized by high exchange and low use value.[94] Thus humans become reduced to commodities and have value only with respect to their utility or exchange value.

Such a view was also articulated by Kant in arguing against prostitution. His ideas compliment nicely the point Marx makes, but from a radically different perspective:

> to allow one's person for profit to be used by another for the satisfaction of sexual desire, to make of oneself an Object of demand, is to dispose over oneself as over a thing and to make of oneself a thing on which another satisfies his appetite, just as he satisfies his hunger on a steak. . . . To let one's person out on hire and to surrender it to another for the satisfaction of his sexual desire in return for money is the depth of infamy. The underlying moral principle is that man is not his own property and cannot do with his body what he will. The body is part of the self; in its togetherness with the self it constitutes the person; a man cannot make of his person a thing.[95]

Kant and Marx essentially agree that such uses of the body are inherently alienating because they destroy the self. Recall Wartofsky's understanding of prostitution as the paradigm of alienation (see chapter 2 above). In making oneself thus available, one becomes a commodity and thus creates a gap between body and self. Consequently, the self ultimately becomes destroyed because one becomes a means and not an end.

While one can argue that Marx utilizes a romanticized understanding of labor and that the concept of labor as a highly creative process might be a figment of Marx's imagination and utterly unrealistic as experienced by modern workers, one can yet use alienation as a way of analyzing labor, especially white collar labor as C. Wright Mills has done.[96]

In preindustrialized societies, individuals traded or sold commodities to each other. In industrialized societies, the workers sell their labor and services. In modern bureaucratized organizations, workers—in particular white collar workers—sell their social personality. This is a consequence of being in a society dominated not only by the market but by a marketing ideology, that is, everything can be sold with the right methods and methods of influence.[97]

In modern bureaucratized society, there are two opposing tendencies: the impersonality of relations because of market influences and the attempt to have people in sales act as if they are personally engaged with the customer. Thus personality traits become commodities on the labor market.

Because the salesperson knows that his or her personality is what influences the sale, he or she experiences the transformation of his or her personality into an instrument designed to generate or secure sales.

> One knows the salesclerk not as a person but as a commercial mask, a stereotyped greeting and appreciation for patronage; one need not be kind to the modern laundryman, one need only pay him; he, in turn, needs only to be cheerful and efficient. Kindness and friendliness become aspects of personalized service of public relations of big firms, rationalized to further the sale of something. With anonymous insincerity the Successful Person thus makes an instrument of his own appearance and personality.[98]

Thus the salesperson becomes alienated from self. Additionally, the customer knows of the instrumentality of the salesperson's personality and serves as a mirror which shows this to the salesperson. But the customer also wishes to hide from the fact that the salesperson is trying to exploit him or her and develops a counter personality to manipulate the salesperson. Thus each are estranged from each other and alienation of the worker and commodification of the person become the norm.

> Men are estranged from one another as each secretly tries to make an instrument of the other, and in time a full circle is made: one makes an instrument of himself, and is estranged from it also.[99]

Thus though contemporary labor differs from the artisan of the preindustrial age and the body-breaking work of early capitalism, it is alienating because of the estrangement it produces because of the commodification of the person through the development of the market personality. Such commodification can affect also the rest of one's life by introducing the suspicion that all interpersonal relations are characterized by such exploitation.

Summary
Alienation in the general sense described by Wolf as a type of disillusionment or disenchantment can be an experience of both the social parents and the surrogate. On the one hand, because the social parents are unable to have a child, they may be alienated

from the society which presently reflects a pronatalist bias. They may experience their marriage as problematic and themselves as useless or unfulfilled because they cannot meet their own desires or the expectations of the culture. On the other hand, the surrogate may be attempting to overcome feelings of alienation that stem from past experiences, for example, of abortion, or from the perception of a lack of contribution to society, or from a sense of not having fulfilled herself as a woman. Thus this broad understanding of alienation is relevant to general motivations that may lead some to seek a surrogate and others to become surrogates.

Second, it is possible for both the surrogate and the baby she carries to be understood primarily in terms of their exchange value and not their use value. That is, both may become commodities, seen as objects to be exchanged on the market. From this perspective, the surrogate is of value only with respect to her reproductive capacity and the child is of value only insofar as it fulfills certain needs for the social parents. Thus, to paraphrase a previous statement of Marx, surrogacy permits things to be sold which were given away or were experienced as part of a personal relationship.

In this context, we need to recall Parker's finding that a commercial transaction was seen as a necessary, but not totally sufficient, reason for becoming a surrogate. Such a transaction, especially if defined contractually, opens the door to the commodification of the surrogate and, more precisely, her reproductive capacities. Essentially what is of value is her biological capacity to produce the desired child of the social parents. She is valued primarily, but not necessarily exclusively, because of her instrumentality in producing a child. The potential for objectifying the surrogate's capacity for reproduction substantially opens the door for the alienation of a capacity that is essentially personal in nature.

Additionally, the child can also be seen as a commodity or reduced to exchange value or to some instrumental means. Fees for expenses incurred during pregnancy are one thing (though even here we may only be talking degrees) but contractual fees for the conception, carrying, birthing, and relinquishment of a child are another thing. While we are not in the situation of surrogacy at the highest offer,[100] nonetheless the child is being placed in a context, if not the actual position, of commodification. If the child is seen as the means whereby a marriage or roles will be fulfilled, then the child is being reduced to a means.

Even though the fee paid to the surrogate is for relinquishment or service, it is very difficult not to see that fee as a payment for the child. This is especially so when the conditions for accepting the child become clearly defined. That is, if the child does not meet certain standards, the fee will not be paid. Were there no fee at all and no conditions on the acceptance of the child by the social parents, the issue of the commodification of the surrogate and child would certainly be reduced in scope and concern. As it is, the suspicion is high that "doing it for the money," to apply Wartofsky's description of participation in research, is alienating an intimate personal/biological process and reducing the surrogate to her biological capacities and alienating her from herself. The child also participates in this alienation by becoming a commodity and a possible instrument in the satisfaction of a variety of needs.

Third, the issue of the market personality is critical. To become a surrogate, an individual must present herself to a variety of people: the director of the surrogate agency (if any), an attorney, sometimes a psychiatrist or psychologist, and the social parents who formally or informally contract with her. To be accepted as a surrogate, the woman must be acceptable to these individuals. This presents a conflict of interest. If the woman wants to be a surrogate, she has the incentive to present herself in the most favorable light. On the other hand, she also has the incentive to minimize or conceal those aspects of herself or background that would make her less presentable or acceptable. Thus she must market her person and personality and expose herself to the risk, if not certainty, of alienation.

A surrogate that I met on a TV talk show was an extremely attractive young woman with a classic peaches-and-cream complexion, set off by marvelous strawberry-blond hair. Much was made of her intelligence, though she admitted not finishing high school. The presence of her husband at her side testified to the stability of her marriage. Their child, who was not on the show, witnessed to her capacity to reproduce successfully and without genetic problems. Her personality was very warm and cheerful, and she appeared to have a comfortable relation with the social parents who sat opposite her on the studio set. All in all, she was the ideal "girl next door."

Yet certain questions kept nagging at me. If she were so intelligent, why didn't she finish high school? Why was she working at a job with no future? Why was she pregnant with someone else's child? Why was her husband so happy with this? These questions are somewhat *ad hominem,* but I think they are important. There seemed to be a gap between the image she was projecting, or was being projected for her, and who she really was. Was her image herself or did she develop a "surrogate personality" so she could successfully market herself or be marketed by others? The truth in this case will not be known, but it raises an issue that needs further reflection. Again, the potential for developing the marketing personality contains the seeds of alienation.

The same issue can also be true for the social parents. They also may be encouraged to market their personalities in such a way as to become acceptable to a potential surrogate, staff of a surrogacy agency, lawyers, and physicians, and so on. By presenting such a marketable personality, they may become alienated from themselves. Thus, even though they may succeed in obtaining the child, they may have also succeeded in changing themselves into individuals they may not recognize.

Unfortunately, data are not available on this issue, but it strikes me that the concept of the market personality is quite relevant to the issue of surrogacy and points to an area of concern. This is an area for inherent conflict of interest between the surrogate and the social parents. Developing a "surrogate personality" and a "social parent personality" based on a variety of personal and social needs could serve to conceal relevant information. It could also help suppress or repress motivating factors that would be of interest. Finally, developing such marketing personalities could be detrimental to all parties concerned because their real selves will be concealed and perhaps altered. Such alienation of self from the self will be detrimental to further psychosocial development and could be harmful to the child.

The commodification of what is personal to one's self, the reduction of persons to exchange relationships, the commodification of the child, and the development of market personalities are all areas of concern. This is an area that needs attending to by the individuals involved in the surrogacy process presently and should be the object of further investigations.

CONCLUSIONS

The issues of family, coercion, and alienation provide significant perspectives from which to view the practice of surrogacy. As seen in the discussion of each of these perspectives, none of them provides a definitive position or resolution of the issues of particular problems in surrogacy. Nonetheless each continues to cast its shadow over the practice.

While I do not want to argue a conservative natural law position that the orders of nature reflect a metaphysical structuring of reality, when we talk about the family—and reproduction—we simply cannot dismiss nature or biology. That is to say, the biological relatedness of the child provides a basis for the relation as well as a specification of the degree of relatedness to others. To dismiss this as insignificant or morally irrelevant is to eliminate a significant aspect of our being. Additionally, as O'Donovan noted, in begetting a child, a relation is established between the procreative and relational goods of marriage. The marriage and the child are both made secure and are socially accepted by the embodiment of the relation in fruitful intercourse.

To argue this position is not to argue that it is exceptionless or that alternative practices are inherently wrong. The position does argue that alternatives to having a child conventionally within heterosexual marriage should be understood as exceptions and that we disregarded the bodiliness of begetting at our peril. Obviously individuals adopt children and do so successfully, and society recognizes this as the good that it is. Gender preference is not an inherent disqualification for adoption and successful parenthood. Yet we see these as exceptions to the norm. We also correctly prefer child rearing in these circumstances to occur within a stable relationship for the good of the child as well as that of the parents-to-be.

Surrogacy biologically steps outside of the embodiment of one relationship and initiates a technical emobdiment of another, even though there is no mutuality in the second other than contractual. The problematic nature of this comes from two aspects. First, the rather total discomfort with establishing a pregnancy with a surrogate through traditional sexual intercourse. Most see this as adultery—and to be prohibited. Assuming no attraction of the husband for the surrogate, has the situation changed morally by substituting a syringe for a penis? Has technology served merely to disguise a problematic extramarital relation which intends to produce a child? Second, genetically the child so conceived has in fact what will be socially denied: multiple relationships. The child inherits—irrespective of choice—the relatives of the surrogate as his or her relatives. The reality of these relations are important for identity both socially and biologically. Yet half of them will be disregarded. Indeed, even the genetic-carrying mother is expected to disappear postbirth. Thus surrogacy departs from our bodiliness in a problematic fashion that serves to disrupt essential relationships.

Coercion is also a critical, although unclear facet of surrogacy. As we have seen, coercion in the technical sense described by Gert is difficult to realize. Perhaps the better term is undue influence. But whether we use the term coercion in a less rigorous way or prefer undue influence, we cannot avoid the implications of differences in class, status, and power in the securing of a surrogate. Money is a prime motivator and few have the expectation that surrogates will perform their duties for nothing. Those surrogates on whom we have some data—and that number is very small—appear to be from lower classes. Those hiring the surrogates have tended to be from the upper classes or to have access to the money necessary to secure a surrogate's services.

Such class, status, and power differentials are disturbing because in themselves they put the surrogate at a disadvantage. She may not, for example, be able to hire her own attorney to advise her on the implications of the contract. Since the common practice is for the rearing mother and genetic-rearing father to pay the attorney, who also secures the surrogate, there may be an inherent conflict of interest against which the surrogate will not be protected. Additionally, the surrogate may think the somewhat standard fee of ten thousand dollars a significant amount of money for her services. But if one calculates the services of the surrogate on an hourly rate during the pregnancy, she is earning less than $1.50 an hour. One can argue that the pregnancy does not interfere with another job she might have and that the pay is a nice supplement. Or, if she does not have a job, she is now ten thousand dollars ahead. While these points are correct, they are also irrelevant. For if the surrogate is working, she will have to take some time off and this may put her job in jeopardy or she may suffer some loss of income. And if she is to consider surrogacy as her job, she is certainly being paid much less than the minimum. In the first instance, the experiential nature of pregnancy is discounted too much and, in the second, the pay scale contributes to the continual trivialization of women and pregnancy.

Differences in class, status, and power between surrogates and those who find them and those who hire them are significant issues. This context may create situations in which surrogates are unduly induced or are in fact coerced. Whether a surrogate is actually coerced can only be determined on a case-by-case basis. That is, I am not persuaded that the situation is inherently coercive. Yet the situation is inherently problematic and needs careful watching.

Alienation with the concomitant danger of commodification of the surrogate and child represents a real danger. Money is exchanged for impregnation and pregnancy and the delivering of the child to the nurturing mother and genetic-nurturing father. There is also a sliding payment scale which adjusts the fee for miscarriages. I do not understand how one can deny this is either the renting or selling of body parts or a child.

One is, in my judgment, taking an intimate personal experience and a body part and attaching a price to them and turning their use over to another. This is the essence of alienation and reduces the surrogate and her body to an object. Additionally, the exchange of cash for the child reduces him or her to a commodity. This is essentially destructive of the person and places the child at the mercy of a contract and the market. This presents the strongest argument against surrogacy thus far. The surrogate and child become instruments in the satisfaction of either a need or a want and so are wronged in their personhood by such reduction to a means.

These three issues suggest that surrogacy is practiced in a context that is inherently problematic. This means that extreme care needs to be given to thought of socially sanctioning its practice. It also means that we need to confront directly as a society the possibility that there may be limits on our desires and even our needs.

·4·

Specific Ethical Issues

Having examined three major thematic moral issues in surrogate motherhood, I now turn to specific ethical concerns. First, I will present several problems that are more background in nature and bear only indirectly on the ethics of the issue. Then I will examine in detail specific ethical arguments about surrogate motherhood.

THEMATIC BACKGROUND ISSUES

Who Is the Surrogate?

The vast majority of the literature on surrogacy assumes that the woman who carries the pregnancy is the surrogate mother. However, as John Robertson notes, "Indeed, it is the adoptive mother who is the surrogate mother for the child, since she parents a child born by another."[1] The woman who contributes egg and uterus functions more as a substitute *spouse* than as a substitute *mother*. Thus the woman who adopts this child is the surrogate mother.

Robinson is unique in making this observation, but he touches on a very critical problem: nomenclature for the various actors and actresses in this drama of pregnancy. The eradication of any relation between biology and social roles complicates matters considerably because it is possible for as many as five different individuals to be involved in the production and rearing of a child. Various schemata of classification attempt to capture the complexity of the issue.

R. and E. M. Snowden and G. Mitchell, for example, propose

the following nomenclature for females and males involved in this process.[2]

I. The Female
1. The *genetic* mother: the one who produces and matures the egg.
2. The *carrying* mother: the one in whose uterus the embryo implants and develops.
3. The *nurturing* mother: the one who cares for the baby after its birth.
4. The *genetic-carrying* mother: the one who supplies the egg and uterus, but does not care for the child after birth.
5. The *genetic-nurturing* mother: the one who produces the egg and will care for the baby after birth, but does not carry the pregnancy.
6. The *carrying-nurturing* mother: the one who carries the pregnancy and cares for the baby after birth but does not supply the egg.
7. The *complete* mother: the one who individually combines all three roles.

II. The Male
1. The *genetic* father: the one who provides and delivers the sperm, whether for internal—which may be physical or artificial—or external fertilization.
2. The *nurturing* father: the one who cares for the baby after birth but was not directly responsible for its inception.
3. The *complete* father: the one who combines the genetic and nurturing roles.

This nomenclature serves two functions remarkably well. First, the suggested names clearly and precisely indicate who is doing what and, occasionally, with whom. Second, it reveals the complexity and possibilities of the reproductive cycle once technology enters that process.

In this schema, the genetic-carrying mother refers to the common understanding of surrogate mother and does so in a way that indicates the typical origin of half the genetic material. My usage in this book is that surrogate mother means genetic-carrying mother. While Robertson's point is certainly worth considering, my judgment is that the literature and common usage is against his suggestion that the nurturing or genetic-nurturing mother be called the surrogate.

Who Is the Mother?

An immediate problem raised by such separation of biology and social roles is the issue of who is the *real* mother? Since there are seven biological/social possibilities, the question is not as silly as it sounds.

The assumption of most of the literature is that the real mother is the nurturing mother, the one who raises the child, irrespective of any biological relation to the child. The notion of motherhood is established through contract or intention, by which the nurturing mother declares her intention to accept and raise the child. This may or may not be followed by a formal adoption of the child by the nurturing mother. This adoption would be out of preference since our culture recognizes only paternity as the determining factor for legitimacy.

The reality is that the issues are a bit more complex than this approach would have us believe. The crass, but biologically accurate, proverb of "Mama's baby, papa's maybe" must now be amended to say "Mama's maybe; papa's maybe; whose is the baby?" For without stringent safeguards, no one can state for sure that the externally fertilized egg or a transferred embryo came from the woman who bears the child. Nor, legally, is it certain that the nurturing mother can claim traditional motherhood. Thus what was once certain, is now debatable, given the possibility of technological intervention.

Motherhood is now divisible. This has rendered moot or at least irrelevant the "irrebuttable presumption that a child born to a married couple is the legitimate offspring of that couple."[3] Biologically, at least two different women in various combinations could lay claim to maternity. Socially, the nurturing mother, who may or may not have some biological relation to the child, may also claim to be the mother. Thus we return to the court of Solomon with different individuals clamoring over who is the mother and whose is the baby. Solomon's solution to determine the real mother was to threaten to cut the disputed child in half and give each of the claimants a half.[4] Is there a less drastic and dramatic solution?

Although typically the surrogate situation involves only the genetic-gestational mother and the nurturing mother, three different women could lay claim to the fact of motherhood in the same pregnancy: the genetic mother who is the source of the egg, the carrying mother who brings the pregnancy to term, and the nurturing mother who will raise the child. The first two have the traditional evidence for biological motherhood and neither of them could "succeed in establishing that the other was not the biological mother."[5] The claim of the nurturing mother is unclear, although the practice of adoption could help support her claim. Thus, in the event of the breach of a surrogacy contract by any party to the contract, determination of motherhood would be difficult to adjudicate and the child's fate would be in jeopardy.

Two authors with radically different philosophies have proposed the same solution to the motherhood problem. George Annas argues that the "current legal presumption that the gestational (or birth mother) is the legal mother should remain."[6] There are two reasons for this. First, there will be a certainty of identification at birth. As George Annas has often noted, if there is anyone who is certainly present at the birth of a child, it is the woman who gives birth to that child. Second, this solution

> recognizes the biological fact that the gestational mother has contributed more of herself to the child than the genetic mother, and therefore has a greater biological investment and interest in it.[7]

Consequently, Annas argues that "the child's father should be presumed to be the husband of the child's mother."[8] Through this argument, Annas hopes to protect the integrity of the family and the interests of the children.

Arguing out of the model of artificial insemination by donor (AID), Oliver O'Donovan argues that the "child belongs to the womb that bore it, irrespective of who the genetic parents are."[9] O'Donovan argues that gamete donation is not parenthood in its fundamental sense.

Gamete donation is possible precisely in order to enable *another* person to become a parent. The husband's parenthood is ensured by his social and sexual relation to his wife, whose own parenthood is given in the fact of her pregnancy—for although she can also claim genetic parenthood, the displacement of the donor makes it clear that genetic parenthood does not matter.[10]

O'Donovan moves this way because of his unhappiness with the consequences of understanding parenthood genetically. First, he recognizes that this opens the door to womb leasing, as he terms it, and to reconsidering gamete donation as a form of adoption. Second, he sees that some type of mathematical formula might have to be used to determine parenthood. For example,

We might say that parental ownership would reside in any couple who, being married or deemed married at the time of the child's conception, contributed between them two out of the three elements necessary to the procreation of a child: either two gametes, or one gamete and the pregnancy.[11]

This solution to parenthood allows AID and womb leasing, but would not allow a combination of womb leasing and ovum donation since the donor would not contribute two out of the three elements. Nor would it permit double gamete donation in which the ovum and sperm both come from donors.

While Annas's concerns for determining motherhood are primarily legal, O'Donovan's are metaphysical.

In the natural order we were *given to know* what a parent was. The bond of natural necessity which tied sexual union to engendering children, engendering to pregnancy, pregnancy to a relationship with the child, gave us the foundation of our *knowledge* of human relationships in this area.[12]

The critical issues for O'Donovan are the tearing asunder of procreation and the reduction of parenthood to a contractual relation. "There will then be no reason to insist that parental ownership should reside in a person who had any physical stake in the child at all."[13] Thus he argues for the child belonging to the womb that bore it as a means of identifying some natural relation with the child. Otherwise there may be no knowing of what a parent is.

To accept Annas's solution, one must accept it as a legal stipulation—even though a recognized one. To accept O'Donovan's solution, one must accept a certain metaphysic. Neither basis may be particularly happy for many people. But both authors point to a critical datum: the centrality of the nine-month gestation period as being morally and/or legally relevant. Minimally, the fact of gestation cannot be dismissed as irrelevant. Maximally, one can argue that gestation is part of a normative order consequent upon certain relations. But in either case the reality of gestation is seen as compelling in determining the woman who gives birth as the mother. Thus the biological mother has the edge in being defined as the real mother. One dismisses biology totally only at great social peril.

The Purpose of Medicine

The primary purpose of medicine is to heal the ill, to intervene to repair a system that is not working properly, or to restore it to its proper state. Medicine performs these tasks by either administering an appropriate medication or treatment or by intervening, surgically or technically. The issue of infertility raises two interrelated questions: Is infertility a disease and what is the nature of medicine?

Infertility is surely the consequence of a malfunction of a biological process or organic system. Large numbers of people experience infertility and suffer distress from the incapacity to have a child. The reproductive technologies of IVF, surrogate motherhood, and embryo transfer respond to this problem.

But several issues arise. First, reproductive technologies resolve the issue of childlessness, not infertility. If one or both of the couple were infertile before IVF, surrogate motherhood, or embryo transfer, they are just as infertile after—even though they have a child. Thus if infertility is a disease, the reproductive technologies do not cure it.

Second, is childlessness a disease? Many individuals suffer immensely and go to great and difficult lengths to have a child. But is it a disease as we would normally understand it? Similarly, is pregnancy a disease? Surely pregnancy has been medicalized, but that does not make it a disease. Childlessness may be a symptom of a malfunction and the frustration of a desire to have children may be traumatic, but does that make it a disease? Neither having a child nor possessing the ability to have a child appears to have anything to do with one's general state of health.

Additionally, we are unclear about whether the experience of wanting a child is a need or a wish. Biologically, having children is necessary for the survival of the society. But that does not mean that each and every member of the society must have a child. As noted earlier, a pronatalist bias is pervasive within our culture and one cannot be totally sure whether or not one's desire is a reflection of a social need, the expression of a biological reality deep within us, the expression of a personal preference, or some indistinguishable combination of all of the above.

Several approaches to this question have been made Both R. G. Edwards, the physician, and Peter Singer, the philosopher, make a similar point when they admit that the reproductive technologies do not cure infertility but add that neither does insulin cure diabetis, intal asthma, nor eyeglasses myopia. Thus, in their perspective, the reproductive technologies are simply yet another means of solving some clinical defect.[14] If the treatment succeeds and the people have their desired children, the treatment has worked. Thus the relief of infertility through nontraditional means stands within the traditional practice of medicine.

In strong contrast to this, Leon Kass argues that infertility is not a disease in a medical sense and that the use of technical means to overcome childlessness is treating a desire, not a pathological condition.[15] This orientation is complimented by the ethicist Paul Ramsey who suggests that a child conceived by IVF is a "prosthesis for his mother's condition."[16] The critical issue is what is one responding to: the satisfaction of a desire or the curing of a disease. For Kass (and Ramsey) the reproductive technologies clearly fall into the satisfaction of desire. Such acts are not acts of medicine but of indulgence or gratification in that they aim at pleasure or convenience or at the satisfaction of some other desire, and not at health.[17]

Surely the debate over health and disease will continue, for the definitions and debate rest on highly controverted philosophical and religious premises. But this debate is an important one, for questions of policy with respect to allocation of resources, research priorities, and even malpractice will be affected by the outcome of the debate. But regardless of whether one views medicine more holistically and inclusive of the patient's life projects or more narrowly restricted to specific interventions to restore a system to its functional integrity, still some approaches can be made that will help in developing an approach to the reproductive technologies.[18]

First, we need to be explicit that such technologies do not cure infertility, but solve the issue of childlessness. While perhaps too obvious a point to make, nonetheless for some individuals the relief of childlessness may not resolve issues related to infertility. Thus care must be taken to determine which issue looms larger for the individual or couple.

Second, when there is a reasonable choice between cure and circumvention, preference should be given to cure. Going the route of traditional curative medicine raises fewer ethical dilemmas. One remains within a generally accepted understanding of how medicine works. And, if successful, one will have restored a capacity to the person. Additionally, efforts to cure may be less socially controversial and may be more likely to receive continued funding.

Third, given the failure of curative medicine, one may turn to compensatory medicine. In essence, while there is nothing wrong with compensatory medicine, nonetheless its practice does raise some issues. One needs to consider the issues of the allocation of resources and where this need fits into policy priorities. Do facts of biological contingency constitute rights or entitlements to care? While such facts—such as infertility—may be unfortunate, do they create a situation of unfairness that society is obligated to remedy?[19]

Thus, while compensatory treatment may not necessarily be

eliminated, one can easily argue that it is not the first choice. After reasonable efforts to cure any underlying pathology have failed, one may turn to compensatory methods. But when one does this, one should not be surprised to find that such methods may be controversial and not supported financially by public or private means of compensation.

The Body as Property

Although this country does have the history of the practice of chattel slavery, legally speaking the body is now not considered to be property.[20] Since the body is not property, an individual cannot will his or her organs or contract for their sale, specific legal provision absent, such as, in the United States, the selling of blood, blood products, and sperm.[21] Given these exceptions, there is strong sentiment and ethical arguments for not viewing the body or body parts as property.

This premise is based on the experience of the dignity of the human and principle of respect for persons.

> This respect is a fundamental requirement of justice, in virtue of which no human being is to be used or exploited for any purpose whatsoever. It is a recognition that individually every human being at least has the right not to be used merely as means to the needs or interests of others and every innocent human being has at least the right not to be killed.[22]

And in commenting on the Kantian dictum distinguishing between things that have a price and things that have a dignity— "If it has a price, something else can be put in its place as an equivalent; if it is exalted above all price and so admits of no equivalent, then it has a dignity"[23]—Thomas Murray notes that pricing of organs leads to their commodification and to profiteering. This violates our cultural sense of specialness about the body and its parts, even when separated from the person.

> And we have certainly recognized that body parts, whatever their dignity, can also have a price. But, on balance, we have rejected the idea that they should be bartered on the market. And we are reluctant to say that whatever interest people do

have in removed organs is a property interest in the usual
sense. We do not let people sell them, nor do we let others
profit unduly from them.[24]

The moral danger of viewing the body as a commodity or as
property is, first, the effect on the dignity and value of the person.
Pricing the body or its parts reduces the body to an entity that
can be exchanged with another commodity. Such pricing suggests
that there is no or little transcendent value to the body or its
parts. This commodification would reduce the body, and with
it, the person to their price on the market. Thus, following Kant's
terminology, the individual would no longer have a value, but
only a price.

Second, such pricing of the body could result in the body's
being alienated. Of concern is the consequence of taking something so intimate to oneself as one's body or a body part and
objectifying it through a pricing mechanism. This severs the relation of one's body with one's self and makes the body an object
over against oneself. Such objectification leads then to an alienation of self from one's totality.

Third, such a pricing system may lead to a distrust of science
and medicine by the public.[25] There may be fears that individuals
will be taken advantage of. Suspicions of conflicts of interest may
interfere with the trust necessary to ensure high quality care.
And individuals may be even more reluctant or unwilling to donate organs, body parts, or their bodies because of the suspicion
that others will profit from one's gift. People may be willing to
make a gift of their bodies as long as it remains a gift. If the gift
becomes commercialized, its value as a gift is destroyed and the
donor is wronged by this change in status.

Having the body retain its status as gift fosters a sense of altruism, maintains respect for human dignity, preserves the integrity of the body-person unity, and encourages a trusting relation between the public and the scientific community. Pricing
or selling the body or body parts reduces them to yet another
commodity for market consumption. Thus alienation can enter
into and destroy one of the most intimate and personal of all
human relations: the self and the body.

The Family
Another area in which surrogacy raises a variety of questions and poses a challenge to traditional ways of thinking and relating is within the family. Surrogacy raises the questions: What is a family, who are members of it, and what expectations do we have of it?

Traditionally, reproduction is important for the constitution of a family because the relations among the members rest on a genetic connection.[26] Such genetic links may be direct as with children to parents or indirect as with children to grandparents or aunts and uncles, and so on. In addition to the genetic dimension, marriage is also important in establishing a family for the "public declaration of marriage removes any confusion about who is related to whom."[27] The genetic and family relations with the partners of the marriage are established by the public ceremony of the marriage. This relation then gives the child and other relatives "a right to have access to other close family members and to have knowledge about them."[28]

Artificial reproduction—whether AID, IVF, surrogate motherhood, or some other method—raises the question: Who is the mother and who is the father?

> That this is not a rhetorical question is clear when we recall that the person so identified is subject to a range of obligations and possesses certain rights, and that these can only be given up or ignored in exceptional circumstances. If more than one kind of mother exists, which shall be given precedence?[29]

The issue is the relation between social/nurturing and biological parenting. Snowdon and his colleagues argue,

> It seems that what we consider as being the most important role of parenthood, namely the nurturing of the child, is insufficient of itself to endow full parent status. The nurturing role may be seen *socially* as the most important but the genetic role is also an essential component, and this is recognized by both parent and child.[30]

The evidence for this position is the direct and indirect relations established by the genetic linkages, the exerting of the power of the genetic link even when absent as through the use of the term "adopted" child, the desire of adopted children to learn the identity of their genetic parent(s), and the necessity for stable and predictable relations within the family to ensure the well-being of children. Artificial modes of reproduction can introduce an element of deception into the family structure, do change the mixture and relation of genetic and nurturing functions, and restructure family relations. Because of the importance of genetic relations within a family and the potential of artificial modes of reproduction to erode this genetic basis and the social rules which support the family, Snowdon argues that the implications for the family may be quite serious.

Also there is concern that

> the intervention of a third party has become, even by comparison with artificial insemination, so direct and all-encompassing that the human bonding which different ethical systems seek to preserve in sex and marriage may be jeopardized.[31]

This concern is complimentary to Snowdon's questions about whether or not artificial means of reproduction may disturb and harm the bonds between the sexes and between parents and children. The point is not that artificial reproduction is "unnatural" in a biological sense, but that the bonds between people, though they change, "require more than a casual fidelity on the part of successive generations."[32]

Clarity about identity and family lineage are related issues and stand behind the traditional prohibitions on incest and adultery. Such practices blur the sharp boundaries inherent within traditional marriage and reproduction. The continuing relation of a surrogate with a child may confuse the child as to who his or her mother really is. Such a relationship may also involve confused perceptions about the actual relations of relatives of the surrogate to the child. Can the surrogate's parents, for example, claim to be surrogate grandparents or demand some sort of visitation privileges with the child based on their genetic link? Also, if the surrogate has another child, could this child be confused or perhaps even threatened by seeing a sibling being given/sold to some other family?[33] And since these children are half siblings, what weight, if any, ought that be given with respect to future relations they may desire?

There have been at least two cases in which one sister has been the surrogate mother for the other. Thus the one sister is simultaneously the genetic-carrying mother and aunt. Will this be confusing to her or, ultimately, to the child? And what about the husbands of each of the sisters? Will they have a new relation with each other and to their wives?

On the one hand, the situation of surrogacy is somewhat analogous to that of a blended family. Here new relations are formed between individuals who are genetic relatives and genetic strangers, so to speak. Because of the genetic unrelatedness there is an asymmetry of relations in surrogate families. Since we already have the experience of difficulties arising from such asymmetry in second marriages, is it unreasonable not to assume that similar difficulties could arise in families formed through the use of surrogates?[34] Others, however, argue that given the range of other issues facing the contemporary family, such issues are minor and pose no genuine threat to the family structure.[35]

The surrogacy situation differs from blended families, though, in that it is intentional. The child is conceived and carried with the clear purpose of placing him or her into another familial context. A traditionally understood blended family is a response to some disruption in the structure of a family unity—divorce or death, for example. One had not, prior to surrogacy, set out intentionally to form blended families. Thus, while one can argue that specific contractual relations may resolve some or all of these issues,[36] nonetheless there is the intentional blurring of traditional genetic relationships, especially if the surrogate maintains a relation with the child and family.

Individuals seeking to resolve childlessness are highly motivated, are willing to undergo many sacrifices, and to expose themselves to the risk of failure to have a child genetically related to one of them. While such a child is not "theirs" genetically, the child is a product of their desire and undoubtedly will be welcomed into a loving, nurturing home. But how biological relations

with the genetic-carrying mother and those genetically related
to her will be resolved remains to be seen. So too does the experience of surrogacy on our understanding of family and marriage. We ignore these issues to the peril of families and children.

SPECIFIC ETHICAL ISSUES

Risks Associated with Surrogacy
    Many of the risks associated with the surrogacy process are
the same as or similar to those associated with many other of the
methods of artificial reproduction, for example, the risks to the
embryo associated with in vitro fertilization or embryo transfer.
There are additional risks associated with egg retrieval, pregnancy, the surrendering of the fetus, and from the social impact
of surrogacy.

Risks to the embryo
    The first confirmed in vitro fertilization occurred in 1959 when
Dr. M. Chang of the Worcester Foundation for Experimental
Biology successfully fertilized a rabbit egg in vitro.[37] By 1971
Edwards and Steptoe had developed a technique for the external
fertilization of human eggs. They also established a method for
the transfer of that fertilized egg into the prepared uterus of a
female so a pregnancy could be established. These developments
were the culmination of a century of work on animal and human
reproductive systems. In 1978 this research culminated in the
birth of the first child conceived in vitro.
    One issue is whether or not there is risk to human embryos
during the process of in vitro conception. Dr. John Biggers, a
reproductive biologist and a consultant to the Ethics Advisory
Board, begins his analysis by observing that embryos produced
in vitro "will show at least the variability that occurs as the result
of natural mating."[38] This means that we can expect about "69
percent of the embryos to be defective and unable to develop to
term if reimplanted in their mothers."[39] Biggers says that the
incidence of abnormalities could occur in four ways: "induction
of chromosome aberrations, increased rate of fertilization by abnormal spermatozoa, induction of point mutations and by physical and chemical teratogens."[40] At the time of this report in 1979,

Biggers determined that superovulation techniques in rabbits and mice produced an increase in the incidence of chromosomal aberrations, that spermatozoa which have not passed through the female genital tract may have an increased risk of becoming abnormal, but that there was no evidence to support the risk of abnormal fertilizations because of point mutations or teratogenic effects because of the techniques used in the procedure.[41] In another review article, in 1981, Biggers summarized the issue of risk from the procedure as follows.

> A considerable amount of experience has accumulated with laboratory and domestic animals on in vitro fertilization and embryo culture, employed separately or in sequence, followed by transfer to surrogate mothers. The combined evidence gives no indication that these techniques cause an increase in the number of abnormal offspring. The issue of whether sufficient work has been done in primates has led to considerable debate.
>
> To summarize, there is evidence that the technique of in vitro fertilization and embryo transfer may increase the incidence of cytogenetic defects in early embryos. . . . When transferred back into the patient's uterus, almost all these embryos can be expected to die, as they do in a natural pregnancy. There is little or no compelling evidence, either experimental or theoretical, suggesting that other types of abnormalities will be increased.[42]

Updated studies show that the techniques present little, if any, risk to mother or fetus. The incidence of congenital defects at birth is about 1 percent and the rate of such abnormalities from these reproductive technologies is identical. An issue of concern is that during the first five years after birth, the detection of abnormalities increases by about 3 percent. Thus continued work needs to be done to determine whether this rate is also present in the babies born of in vitro fertilization. But at present the risks of the present procedure are slight.

Another issue with respect to the embryo is the risk of not being born. That is, does the procedure of in vitro fertilization and/or embryo transfer produce a higher than expected number of miscarriages? First, the fertilization failure rate of the best available in vitro techniques approximate what is experienced naturally, a failure rate of about 15 percent. Thus both natural and artificial methods appear to be equally efficient with respect to establishing fertilization. But, second, what is the probability of the fertilized egg coming to term? Not all of the 85 percent of eggs thus fertilized survive. Total embryonic and fetal loss is quite high; only about 45 percent of ova fertilized in vivo achieve implantation.[43] Data compiled by Grobstein and others show that 1,110 embryo transfers led to "184 pregnancies—a success rate of 17 percent."[44] Thus embryo transfer in IVF is only about 40 percent as successful as the natural process. The rate can be varied somewhat depending on whether one calculates the pregnancy rate per laparoscopy or per embryo transfer. But however one calculates, the probability of success is low.

A final risk is that of an ectopic pregnancy, or the establishment of a pregnancy outside the uterus. Grobstein reports that of 184 pregnancies, 20 were ectopic. This is within the range of ectopic pregnancies for the natural process: 0.3 to 3 percent. This is also below the rate for pregnancies achieved "following tuboplasty to overcome more complex forms of oviductal blockage."[45]

With respect to risks to the embryo or fetus, the procedures of IVF and embryo transfer appear to present no risks greater than those of the natural process of impregnation. The only difference is the difference between success rates of the natural process and IVF. IVF is 40 percent less successful than the already low natural success rate. Thus the artificial process exposes the embryo to a higher risk of the probability of miscarriage. The consensus of many is that such risks are comparable enough to the natural pregnancy rates and maternity risk rates as to be ethically acceptable.[46]

On the other hand, several concerns are raised about this argument. First, Paul Ramsey argues that we cannot perform experiments on unconsenting subjects.[47] Although the argument assumes that the fertilized egg has moral standing in the community and that the procedures are indeed experimental, nonetheless it is clear that the desired outcome is a human child. If not a person, the fertilized egg is at least a patient in a therapeutic procedure or the subject of a research project. As such, some consideration must be paid to the rights of this entity as either a patient or subject.

Second, although there is a high degree of fetal loss in nature, that in itself does not provide sufficient justification for Leon Kass to allow it in the laboratory, Stillbirths, Kass argues analogously, are not a justification for infanticide.[48] Similarly, though famines, earthquakes, and droughts occur and though indeed they are natural occurrences, this does not justify their replication for whatever reason.

Third, when dealing with those already born, we permit them to be used to benefit another *only* when they consent to this process. Similarly, it is only in the rarest circumstances that we permit those who cannot consent to provide benefits for the interests of others. Organ transplants from incompetents to a healthy sibling provide the primary precedent, and it is a highly controversial one.[49] Should one think of conceiving an infant to satisfy the desire of a couple or individual to have a child, as legitimate or as understandable as that may be, as reducing this child to a means to an end? Does such a procedure depart too far from our established and strongly held tradition of respect for human dignity, of prohibiting human subjects from being used as means only?

The argument is that we must be prepared to take new risks associated with artificial reproduction because we have taken risks with natural or traditional conception. This suggests to O'Donovan that

> we must loose all sense of difference between nature and artifice, between the constraints which are given to us as natural conditions for our lives, and the liabilities of projects which we have freely undertaken and might as freely not have undertaken.[50]

Such an orientation leads us to see all of life as instrumental, to blur the distinction between natural and artificial, and to see childbearing as another project which can be realized more efficiently through technique than through natural means. O'Donovan argues,

There is a world of difference between accepting the risk of
a disabled child (where that risk is imposed on us by nature)
and ourselves imposing that risk in pursuit of our own purposes.[51]

Thus desire needs to be qualified by biology, at least to some
extent. While not normative in a metaphysical sense, biology sets
a context in which careful decisions must be made. We are neither
totally subservient to nor totally independent of our bodiliness.
An area of qualification is that of imposing risks of our choosing
on others who are not a party to the decision.

Risks to the child
The child born of this procedure is also exposed to several
risks. The first risk is to the child's identity and development that
may come from exposure to various media. The risks here relate
to the novelty of the situation, the age of the child, how the parents handle the situation, and how this individual will be followed
as a continuing news story. While the novelty issue is somewhat
resolved by the growing numbers of children born through such
techniques, stories frequently appear when a new clinic has its
first success. Such publicity is necessary for the clinic and continues to feed into alleged public interest in these technologies.
Clearly the babies will be unaware of their status and situation.
Certainly Louise Brown did not know she was the cover story of
most major news magazines. When they enter the public arena,
however, renewed attention may be given them. Thus how these
children do in school, for example, may be followed quite closely
and they may be subject to many interviews and exposed to various pressures that may be stressful to them.

Children of the surrogate may also be exposed to stress because
of similar exposure to the media. Individuals may wish to find
out how the surrogate's children feel about their mother's new
role and their surrogate half-sibling.

This situation is complicated because attention should be paid
to all these children so that the consequences, if any, of the mode
of conception, gestation, or rearing and their implications on all

parties can be determined. This will ensure that the children will be singled out to some degree. However, a minimal sense of ethics requires that we follow the results of artificial reproduction so any detrimental effects can be discovered and corrected or eliminated. Such studies should, of course, be carried out in the least intrusive manner possible.

What the parents do with the situation is unpredictable, and it is quite questionable whether they can or ought to be prohibited from doing certain things. Many parents of IVF children, surrogate mothers, and the nurturing parents of children born of various reproductive technologies have written books, magazine articles, and made television appearances describing their experiences. Surely these appeal to a broad public interest in these technologies and can also help to explain these technologies and offer hope or direction to other childless couples. Yet in this there is the danger of the exploitation of the child, the commodification of the experience of the child-rearing process, and placing various expectations on the child with respect to educational, social, or interpersonal skills. Too much publicity may interfere with the already complex process of the child's personality development.

Finally, such artificial means of reproduction may confuse the child's lineage. On the one hand, separation of the child from the gestational mother is not a new phenomenon. The history of adoption gives testimony to the successful rearing of children by individuals not biologically related to the child. Surrogate parenting may fall into that model. On the other hand, many individuals who are adopted or conceived through artificial insemination by donor wish to know the identity of their biological parents. Additionally, if the surrogate maintains a personal relation with the nurturing parents or is related genetically to one of them, there may be confusion about who is related to whom and how. There also may be problems arising from fused roles such as mother-aunt, father-brother-in-law, or other possible combinations. While the experience of blended or AID families may provide a model for some possibilities brought about by the birth technologies, they provide little illumination for the significance, if any, of such fused genetic roles.[52]

Risks to the woman

The question of risk is either relatively straightforward or complicated, depending on who is involved in which procedures. For example, if the surrogate is to be artificially inseminated, the risks relate primarily to infection, ectopic pregnancy, and pregnancy. If an egg is to be harvested from one woman and given to another, then the risks associated with retrieval need to be examined. Additionally, a woman seeking the services of a surrogate will probably have been determined to be infertile and the determination of that status has procedures which carry certain risks. Thus the risks a woman is exposed to is a function of what procedure(s) she undergoes. I will describe several of these.

Infertility work-ups, in addition to the invasion of privacy and removal of intimacy from every aspect of one's sexual relations, typically require an endometrial biopsy. This is a scraping of the uterus with a sharp instrument and an examination of the recovered tissue to determine whether or not the woman is ovulating properly. Next is tubal insufflation, the filling of the oviducts with carbon dioxide to determine whether or not the tubes are open. The uterus and oviducts are examined for structural irregularities by inserting a dye into them and x-raying the structure. There may also be hormonal treatments to help various systems function correctly. Further, the Fallopian tubes may be blown out with liquid to ensure their staying open. Finally, surgery may be necessary to correct various problems. These procedures are painful, the morbidity associated with them may have a negative influence on fertility, and they may need to be repeated frequently.[53]

Second, if egg donation or embryo transfer is part of the surrogacy process, additional risks are incurred. Hormonal treatment to ensure superovulation may cause ovarian cysts. The eggs are retrieved through laparoscopy, a surgical procedure which requires general anesthesia. The uterus can be harmed by the catheter used to reimplant the embryo. The pregnancy is typically monitored through amniocentesis and ultrasound. Amniocentesis carries a very small risk of spontaneous miscarriage. Ultrasound has no known risks at present, but since this is a relatively new procedure, studies should be done to validate its safety. Finally, there is the risk of an ectopic pregnancy following embryo transfer.[54] One must also ask whether or not the low probability of obtaining a live birth following IVF should also count as a risk factor. And when a pregnancy is established, one must also take into account the risk factors associated with it. Because such a pregnancy is often determined to be a high risk pregnancy, delivery may be by Caesarean section, thus presenting additional surgical and anesthetic risks to the mother.

This listing of the risk factors, which in many cases are technically low, does not take into account the pain, suffering, anguish, and crushed expectations that women in particular and their partners experience when these procedures either singly or jointly do not produce the expected result. The suffering consequent upon failure to establish a pregnancy is incalculable except in individual terms, but surely stands as a major issue to be dealt with. It must be considered a risk factor associated with IVF or surrogate motherhood.

That the risks, discomforts, and perhaps morbidity associated with pregnancy are significant is indirectly testified to by Noel Keane in his argument in the *Carey* case which prohibited payment to surrogates. Keane states that "the services of a surrogate mother are *far too onerous* to be provided gratuitously in all but the most unusual cases."[55]

Is There a Right to Have Children?

Many of the arguments justifying the use of surrogates assume or are based on a critical issue: the legal and/or ethical right of a couple to have a child.

A background issue is whether desire can give rise to rights. It is obvious that individuals desire children. It is likewise obvious that having children is a biological capacity associated with the majority of individuals. But does a customary biological capacity and strong personal desire give rise to a legal or ethical claim that one is entitled to a child? No theory of rights can be credibly so based. Such a perception of rights can be described as a "fetishization of specifically biological traits"[56] which turns our attention from moral claims to desired biological capacities.

Alternatively, Ruth Hubbard understands the right to have a child only as a payoff to the woman for having paid her dues of second-class citizenship. Having a baby is the compensation for not being able to do what one would have liked to do. In this sense, not being able to have a baby is a denial, a bargain unfilled. In this context, and this context only, Hubbard states that she can understand a right to artificial means of reproduction. But she also recognizes that this is an affirmation of a sexist status quo which she rejects.[57] Arguments for a right to bear a child are unacceptable for they require that women continue to remain in their subservient social situation.

From a legal perspective, the state has the power indirectly to regulate procreation by its prohibitions on incestuous marriages, its establishment of health requirements, age limitations, and the prohibition of simultaneous polygamy.[58] Additionally, the state can prohibit a citizen's exercise of his or her reproductive powers if the requirements of due process and equal protection are met. These powers, found in *Bell* and *Skinner*,[59] include mandatory sterilization to prevent the transmission of socially injurious tendencies.

There are also constitutionally protected rights relating to procreation based on privacy. Such rights include the right to marry and to have or not to have children. These rights are fundamental and can be overridden only by another fundamental interest such as health of citizens and risks to mother and child.[60] It seems, then, following John Robertson that

> a likely implication of these cases, supported by rulings in other cases, is that married persons (and possibly single persons) have a right to bear, beget, birth and parent children by natural coital means using such technological aids (microsurgery and in vitro fertilization, for example) as are medically available. It should follow that married persons also have a right to engage in noncoital, collaborative reproduction, at least where natural reproduction is not possible. The right of a couple to raise a child should not depend on their luck in the natural lottery if they can obtain the missing factor of reproduction from others.[61]

This line of reasoning is also followed by Noel Keane. He too argues for a zone of privacy surrounding personal decisions concerning marriage, contraception, family relations, and child rearing and education. From this it follows that the right of privacy means freedom from unwarranted governmental intrusion "into matters which fundamentally affect a person, such as the decision whether to bear or beget a child."[62] While Keane ultimately uses this to justify payment to surrogates, such reasoning establishes, in Keane's judgment, the right of an individual to beget or bear a child, irrespective of means.

Sharon Steeves argues that *Roe* v. *Wade*[63] is the more critical case for the right to artificial reproduction because *Roe* defines privacy in terms of liberty of action, not merely freedom from government interference or observation. Thus

> As long as there is a judicially determined constitutional privacy right which concerns unexpressed but nonetheless fundamental human activities, constitutional access to the means of artificial reproduction seems assured as a logical interpretation of *Roe* v. *Wade*.[64]

This same point is also argued by Kathryn Lorio who says that the decision to beget a child is a protected area of privacy and that "presumably the actual method of begetting also would have to be protected."[65] Thus a statute regulating this area would have to serve a fundamental interest and regulate the activity by the least restrictive means.

It seems reasonable to assume, either as a working assumption or a reality, that there is some sort of legal right to reproduction. It is also clear that there are areas of reproductive life where the government may not interfere, for example, in the use of contraceptives or in an individual's liberty of action in certain instances, for example, first trimester abortions. There is certainly ground here for extending this reasoning to the use of artificial means of reproduction.

But what the law gives, the law also restrains. That is, even a constitutional right can be infringed upon given the showing of a sufficiently compelling state interest.[66] Such interests could be the risks to mother and/or fetus or child, the health of the citizens, or the perception that these new reproductive technologies raise legal problems that admit of no or only problematic solutions. Additionally, the state can restrain artificial reproduction by refusing to provide public money for research or clinical applications. Or the state could refuse to apply or extend existing legislation such as that affecting paternity, maternity, or legitimacy to these new reproductive areas. Such indirect restraints are more easily justified when the reproductive rights in question are negative rights rather than positive rights. That is, if the reproductive right in question is negative, the state has the obligation to ensure only that no one will interfere with individuals as they pursue their rights. Whereas, if the right in question were positive, the state would have an obligation actively to assist in securing the realization of that right. Since many of the rights surrounding reproduction are negative, one may reasonably claim a right to have a child, even by artificial means. But one may not claim that, because of this right, someone—physician or state—must assist one in achieving this goal.

In some respects we stand at an impasse here. The law and constitutional rights define a zone of reproductive privacy that reasonably can be extended to include at least some freedom in the choice of means by which one reproduces. Yet if this is only a negative right, one cannot claim the assistance of others in achieving a pregnancy and child. Present federal policy reflects this situation by finding that research involving human in vitro fertilization and embryo transfer is in essence ethical but has not provided any federal funding for such research.[67] Also there is debate over whether having a child is a need or a want. If there is a biological need for each individual to have a child, then it is easier to justify and mandate efforts to help infertile individuals achieve a pregnancy. However, if having a child is a desire, then there may not be as much urgency or sense of obligation in providing a pregnancy. This is not to deny or minimize an individual's desire to have a child. Clearly people strongly desire children, and their lives are frequently disrupted or experienced as incomplete if they cannot do this.

Nonetheless, desire alone, no matter how intense, does not constitute an ethical or legal claim. Developments in law have helped show how privacy, not need, can and should be understood to include reproductive rights. Others argue that the need alone should constitute a moral justification for both a child and assistance in achieving this. However, an ethical claim transcends in some fashion both biology and desire. If ethics is based exclusively on either of these, we remain prisoners of biology and subjectivity. While both of these realities are important in gaining a deeper understanding of the person, neither are sufficient in themselves to constitute a full or adequate understanding of the human person and his or her ethical claims.

Presently the practice of artificial reproduction frequently evades the whole issue of rights. Infertility is defined as a technical problem for which there is a solution. There is a need and, out of compassion, one responds clinically to this need. By appealing to the traditional practice of medicine, one can avoid the issue of rights all together. The problem is a technical one and there is a technical solution. "The goal, quite simply, is to permit large numbers of previously infertile couples to have their *own* children."[68] Artificial reproduction thus becomes another value-free option of clinical medicine. All other discussions are simply variations on this theme.

Thus in practice the service is provided to those who can afford it, assuming that the extant constitutional framework at least does not prohibit the practice of medicine and that privacy is a right broad enough to cover the desire to have children and the means by which one does this. Thus clinical practice begs the question of whether there is a moral right to do this. Until that question is resolved, any further discussions rest on less than solid ground.

Such a question becomes even more complex when one argues that one has a right to reproduce on behalf of someone else. It is one thing to say that I have a right to use various technologies to assist me in becoming pregnant. It is quite another to argue that my right to have a child entitles me to secure in some fashion the services of another individual to establish a pregnancy through some technical means, carry, and bear a child on my behalf. The argument that all parties involved are simply exercising liberty rights and acting of their own free choice does not respond to the issue of entitlement or the moral question of whether one ought do this. Typically, we do not argue that one is entitled to create another human being as a means of securing a right of one's own. The exercise of such rights reduces the child to a means. Also the surrogate faces the risk of reduction to a means, even though the choice may be voluntary. Establishing a right to have a child via a surrogate is difficult to do because of the involvement of others who may be reduced to means rather than respected as ends.

Compensation for the Surrogate

One of the major issues of contention in the debate over surrogates is whether or not they should be compensated for their service. The debate on this is exceptionally sharp and, as usual, raises fundamental issues.

Reasons for compensation

The first reason is that although adoptions are prohibited by all groups other than a licensed agency, such restrictions do not apply to surrogacy because "bars to or restrictions on independent adoptions do not apply to blood relatives."[69] Because of the child's biological relation to the father, one can argue that any surrogate arrangements should be free of traditional restrictions on adoption or should fall within existing statutory exemptions.

Second, adoption legislation is aimed, in part, at prohibiting baby selling. Such statutes forbid payment for adoption and allow fees only for interim support or agency processing fees. These statutes do not apply to the surrogacy situation. First, the statutes prohibit payment only when adopting. Since the surrogate is not adopting, the statutes do not apply. The biological father is the natural father of the child and takes his child into his family. Second, the evils which the statutes are designed to stop are not present in the surrogacy situation. The child, for example, is not intended to be treated as a commodity or property. The parents desire the child and are not going to turn around and trade the child for something else.[70] Additionally, the surrogate is not being coerced into selling the child. The agreement is voluntary. Third, payment is not for the child, but for the services rendered. The child is not purchased, but the woman is reimbursed for her expenses, her time, and her services. Thus the child is not purchased, rather services are procured.[71]

Third, prohibiting payment to a surrogate to obtain a child may interfere with "a right of personal privacy which includes 'the interest in independence in making certain kinds of important decisions.'"[72] Thus the right of privacy which prohibits interferences in reproductive acts could be extended or understood to encourage surrogates to charge a fee. Prohibitions on charging or paying a fee may "prohibit the exercise of a protected right."[73]

Fourth, prohibiting fees may drive the practice underground. If people are desperate enough for a child, they may be likely to ignore any prohibitions in their desire to achieve their end. Additionally, if the practice is driven underground, any appropriate public scrutiny will be impossible or exceptionally difficult.[74]

Fifth, sperm vendors are in effect paid surrogate fathers. While such individuals are not paid much, they are paid. If a woman who chooses to provide an ovum or uterus cannot be paid for this similar service, this differential treatment is discrimatory.[75] Justice and the "Equal Protection Clause of the Fourteenth Amendment require that the government treat similarly situated individuals in a similar manner."[76]

Finally, if no payment is offered for surrogacy, few may do it.

> Pregnancy and childbirth are hazardous, time-consuming, painful conditions which few women can be expected to experience for the sake of someone else unless they receive meaningful compensation.[77]

Thus some incentive is needed, and until the situation of surrogates is made similar to sperm vendors and meaningful compensation is provided, few surrogates can be expected to come forward. Recall that in Philip Parker's study of surrogates that the perceived need and desire for money were listed first in the motivational factors.[78]

Arguments against compensation

Arguing against compensating a surrogate could seem like arguing against several main components of our economic system: the compensation of one for a service provided, denying someone an opportunity to earn money, and a violation of freedom. Nonetheless there are several substantive concerns with respect to compensation.

The primary way into the payment question is through analogies with adoption. Typically, adopting parents may pay for the medical expenses, and occasionally the rent and food expenses, incurred by the mother.[79] Additionally, the agency receives payments for its services. Thus, the argument goes, paying a surrogate is not buying a baby, but compensating her for her services.

Is the analogy with adoption valid? Herbert Krimmell argues that it is not. Adoption involves the transfer of responsibility from one set of parents to another, but Krimmell argues that this differs from the surrogacy situation for two reasons. "First, it is difficult to imagine anyone conceiving children for the purpose of putting them up for adoption."[80] Thus adoptions usually occur because the conception was undesired or because of problematic circumstances which arise after the birth. Typically the conception was not planned or the postbirth circumstances were not envisioned at the time of conception. Second, Krimmell argues that "not all offerings of children for adoption are necessarily moral."[81] The examples he provides are parents offering their child because they are bored with parenting or because the child is the wrong gender. Even though the justification for the adoption is altruistically stated as bringing happiness to someone else, the child may not be desired for its own sake. Something is desired from it.

There is a second way in which the analogy with adoption fails. This is the prohibition, in many states, of the invalidiity of a prebirth adoption release signed by the mother.[82] And even if not expressly prohibited by law, the burden of proving the validity of such a prebirth agreement falls on the party who wishes to uphold it. As well, the mother need not provide actual evidence of coercion to have the prebirth surrender declared invalid.[83] Since surrogacy is premised on such a prebirth adoption release, this invalidates its major premise.

Thus to conceive a child without wanting it is a departure from our understanding of adoption and changes how we look at children. This practice would see children as objects of manufacture or of utility. The analogy of surrogacy with adoption essentially fails.

Second, the constitutional right to privacy has been invoked as the basis for allowing the surrogate to receive a payment for her services. However, a Michigan court ruled that the state's interest in

> preventing commercialization from affecting a mother's decision to consent to the adoption of her child, thereby adversely affecting the best interests of the child, clearly outweighed any right of privacy that might exist between the contracting parties.[84]

Third, the constitutional provision that seems relevant to the issue of compensation, according to Angela Holder, is not privacy but the Thirteenth Amendment's prohibition of slavery, the sale of one person by another.

> Whether payment was made before the woman is inseminated or after the baby is born seems irrelevant; the intention of the arrangement is to fulfill a contract for the payment of money in exchange for a human being.[85]

Indeed, there is a valid distinction between paying someone for services provided and the outright buying of a baby. But this line seems to be crossed when the surrogates studied define economic compensation as their prime motivation and when one of the leaders in the attempt to legalize surrogacy recognizes that without economic compensation there may not be enough surrogates. Thus children become commodities; the payment is not for the service but the child.

Other arguments against compensation emerge from feminist concerns. If one enters a surrogate contract, for example, there is a strong tendency to view the woman's body, or at least the uterus, as a form of property over which the adopting individual or individuals have control. Such a view is reinforced by contract provisions which frequently regulate the surrogate's diet, exercise, use of drugs, and so on. While the intent may not be to define the woman as property, the consequence is surely to experience her in that fashion.

Additionally, some argue that since no one is forcing the surrogate to engage in this activity, she is simply exercising her freedom of choice. After all, echoing *Roe* v. *Wade*, they claim it's her body and she can do with it what whe wants. Andrea Dworkin argues that

> the bitter fact that the only time that equality is considered a value is in a situation like this where some extremely degrading transaction is being rationalized. And the only time that freedom is considered important to women as such is when we're talking about the freedom to prostitute oneself in one way or another.[86]

In Dworkin's perspective, freedom is seen as socially valuable for women by the dominant social forces only in contexts in which they are involved in selling their bodies in some form. Few people, she notes, argue with equal passion that women ought to be free to be surgeons, bankers, candidates for national office, or the like. The argument that the selling or renting of one's body is an act of the woman's free will attempts to stand apart from the culture or society in which the woman exists. Thus

> In both prostitution and surrogate motherhood . . . the state has constructed the social, economic and political situation in which the sale of some sexual or reproductive capacity is necessary to the survival of the woman. It fixes her social place so that her sex and her reproductive capacity are commodities.[87]

In this perspective freedom is reduced to one dimension: the capacity to buy and sell. And while this is certainly a dimension of freedom, it neither exhausts its possibilities nor is it the most profound expression of freedom. If such an understanding of freedom were to be forced on males, severe resistance would be forthcoming.

Finally, being paid to be a surrogate can be seen as a new type of prostitution.

> Women can sell reproductive capacities the same way old-time prostitutes sold sexual ones but without the stigma of whoring because there is no penile intrusion. It is the womb, not the vagina, that is being bought; this is not sex. It is reproduction.[88]

This is clearly a strong allegation, but it has its point. What "saves" surrogacy from being an act of prostitution, or adultery for that matter, is that a syringe, not a penis, is used for insemination. This may be a distinction with only a modest difference.[89] For the essence of prostitution is not simply the physical insertion of a penis into a vagina, but rather the alienation of the woman's body from herself and the alienation of affection that occurs when one is married or in a significant relation with another. A strong case can be made that surrogacy is another example of self-alienation because of the objectification of one's reproductive capacity. The alienation of affection may not be as easy to demonstrate because the sperm vendor may not have a relation, even minimal, with the surrogate. Yet one has to wonder about the alienation of affection on the part of his spouse consequent upon his desperation to have a child that drives him to rent the uterus of another woman and artifically inseminate one of her eggs.

The issue of compensation is a complex one. We have a tradition of compensation for services and economic motivations are important in our culture. Nonetheless, such considerations must be understood with regard to the social situation of women within our culture and as they serve to reinforce the status quo.

The Interests of the Child

In discussions of surrogate parenthood, because the child is desired and will be welcomed into the home of the biological father and adopting mother, the assumption is that the interests of the child are being protected. Further, the typical contract provides, inasfar as possible, for appropriate prenatal care for the surrogate. Thus the medical interests of the child are attended to.

Some interests of the potential or actual child still remain to be dealt with. Adopted children have expressed a desire to know their biological family of origin.[90] Children born of surrogates might also have this interest. One can argue that this problem need not arise. The child simply need not be told, especially since the child is genetically related to the father. Yet the potential for knowledge of one' origins exist. The child may not have a genetic disease the parent or parents have. The child may also be infertile and the parents could tell the child of his or her own origins to help resolve the problem. The parents may feel a need for honesty in their relation and simply tell the child as many parents who adopt do.

The child who knows of his or her origins may want to know his or her genetic or birth mother. For this interest to be realized, records need to be maintained. At present, some surrogates are known to the rearing parents and some maintain a relation with the new family postbirth. Such relations are not mandated, however. Additionally, if the sperm also came from a vendor or donor, more often than not his identity is unknown. Attention needs to be paid to the interest of the child in knowing his or her full genetic identity. The interest of knowledge of one's genetic identity has implications for record keeping and for evaluating what the rearing parents might tell their child. And this interest has the potential to complicate the relations between the genetic mother (and genetic father) and the rearing family.

While in some ways the issues of the interests with respect to genetic identity of the child are easier to resolve by ignoring them, nonetheless they are real, and denial may only force them to show up at another time and place and cause severe damage to the child and his or her relation with the rearing parents. The child's interests may be harmed by being born with a deprivation with respect to his or her identity.[91]

The child also has an interest in being conceived in a manner as risk free as possible. Whether this interest is also a right is clouded by the debated moral status of the fetus. Minimally, however, we can argue that there is an interest in being so conceived. And, fortunately, the evidence provided by several years of experience has shown that children so conceived have not been harmed by the process. This may be explained by luck, by the screening of the surrogate and sperm vendor, the safety of the procedures used, the enforcement of prenatal contracts, and by selective abortion. But the fetus does not appear to be at any greater risk of harm in being conceived artificially than customarily.

Such an interest may require that the issue of the regulation of clinics be rethought. Presently there are no regulations with respect to licensing, training, or laboratory standards. Since the egg, sperm, and conceptus are subject to a variety of manipulations, the interest of the conceptus in being born in a risk-free manner may require the establishment and maintenance of standards. The fact that no unfortunate events have happened as a consequence of the mode of reproduction is no reason to ignore the health and safety interests of the conceptus.

The conceptus also has at least an interest in not being used as a means to an end. The issue here is a difficult one because it deals with motivation. While not every child born is a wanted child, assumedly most people who have children desire them. And, given contraception, more and more children are being born of desire, not biological necessity, custom, or social pressure.

The concern is whether the welfare of the child or the desires of the parents to have one is paramount. This question is further complicated by the issue of payment and the allegation of baby buying. Thus the issue of the potential commodification of the child is raised again. If the desires of the rearing parents are paramount, the child may be understood instrumentally as a means to satisfy those desires. Such an understanding may put the child into a different perspective and place many expectations on him or her.

The concern is a difficult one, for parents typically do not want a child for the purpose of abusing it. Thus the child is conceived with certain expectations about his or her welfare. And, again typically, children are born of desire. But are such expectations and desires complicated by means of noncoital reproduction, by the contracts made with the surrogate, and the concern over baby selling? The potential for commercializing conception and commodifying the child again pose a concern. The child has an interest in being wanted for himself or herself, not as a means to someone else's ends. Care should be taken that such interests of the child not be ignored or discounted because of the overwhelming desire of the couple to have a child.[92]

The Commodification of the Child

A serious concern thematic to the artificial reproduction revolution is that of the commodification of the child. Specifically, the question is raised in the context of the transfer of money between surrogate and rearing parent(s), regardless of motive. But the more general context also alerts us to some other dimensions. The whole area has been commercialized. It is not unthought of, for example, to have patent applications for specific techniques.[93] Quality control over the developing fetus is maintained through screening procedures. The contract with the surrogate may help establish a product's liability claim. Such issues give rise to the necessity of taking seriously the potential for the commodificiation of the child.

The primary reason for prohibiting the sale of children is to prevent their being viewed as commodities that can be purchased, sold, returned, and exchanged. Such a posture is in line with the current prohibition, with the exception of blood and sperm, on the sale of body parts. The prohibition inhibits our viewing the body, body parts, or, in this case, children, as means to ends and not as valuable entities in themselves. Selling a child, then, devalues it by capitalizing on its potential or actual human worth.

Noel Keane argues that the process of commercialization is simply generalizing what we do in almost all other sectors of our lives. "In a commercial society, 'commercialization' is the usual way in which many individual needs are satisfied."[94] Several responses can be made to this. First, the fact that we buy and sell many things, does not justify buying and selling everything. Second, the position assumes that having children is a need and, therefore, it can be satisfied like other needs. Third, one cannot argue from the fact that some things are sold to the policy that all things ought to be for sale or governed by market considerations.

There are many economic considerations around the experience of pregnancy. Obstetricians, the manufactures of children's clothing and furniture, pediatricians, hospitals, adoption agencies, and private schools clearly all have an economic interest in children. So do parents. Children have been, and in primarily rural areas, still are critical to the economic survival of the family and are a form of social security for their parents. Such practices do not, however, justify buying a child to realize these interests. It is one thing to be born into a family unit and participate in all the activities of that family. It is quite another to be purchased to achieve certain ends.

Arguments developed by George Annas against the sale of frozen embryos can also be applied to the sale of embryos in a surrogate's uterus. There should be no rights of ownership in the embryo because of the possibility of generalizing the practice.[95] But more interestingly, Annas argues that provisions in the Uniform Commercial Code (UCC) show why the sale of embryos or children should be prohibited. Section 2–601 reads:

> if the goods or the tender of delivery fail in any respect to conform to the contract, the buyer may (a) reject the whole; or (b) accept the whole; or (c) accept any commercial unit or units and reject the rest.[96]

Likewise, section 2-604 reads:

> if the seller gives no instructions within a reasonable time after notification of rejection, the buyer may store the rejected goods for the seller's account, or reship them to him, or resell them for the seller's account.[97]

The absurdity of a surrogate contract becomes rather clear even from a benign reading of the UCC. Annas notes that provision (c) would have particular implications for multiple births and forces the issues of the ownership of the unwanted or undesired siblings. Given the sophisticated monitoring of a pregnancy that can occur from the obtaining of the egg and sperm, applying such provisions to a contract to bear and buy a child is not an exercise in rhetoric. What is the fate of the child commissioned under contract if he or she does not meet the terms or expectations of the buyer? One child born under contract has already been rejected,[98] and although the Baby M case was resolved mainly in favor of the Sterns, that does not prevent other similar claims from being brought.[99]

Having a child under contract and/or buying it reduces the child to the status of other objects that we buy and sell. It will have the cash value we assign to it and will be dealt with according to the terms of the contract. The child could be returned if not the kind or type that was desired. In addition to the complications from the Uniform Commercial Code, we must also think of products' liability laws which could be a further basis for the refusal or rejection of a child if it did not have the characteristics one wanted.

Implications of Surrogacy

Introduction

Adolus Huxley's *Brave New World,* first published in 1932, probably contains the most dramatic and comprehensive account of everyone's worst fears of artificial reproduction. Because it presents such an extreme scenario, its substantive criticisms have not been taken that seriously. Yet we should pause in considerable wonderment when we recognize that almost all of the technologies in *Brave New World* are in place or being rapidly developed. The scale on which Huxley's technologies are practiced is missing, as well as their sociopolitical context. But this may be only a matter of time. The mind boggles, though, at Huxley's accuracy. And even though the birth technologies are not widespread and highly utilized, the current practices do have implications that should be considered.

It must be admitted that many of the implications and considerations that will be discussed have no demonstrable answer. On the one hand, the practice is not large enough for a useful study. Yet on the other, if the practice grows, problems may be discovered only after it is too late to provide a remedy. My concern is not to present a series of "worst case" scenarios and then condemn the practice on the basis of those. Rather, I wish to indicate areas of potential problems and ask that they be considered before we rush forward into the unknown. The traditional American practice is to implement a technology and ask questions later, if at all. In fact, this is what we are presently doing with surrogacy. My concern is to draw attention to potential problem areas and consider them before the practice is fully implemented. As Richard McCormick and the late André Hellegers said:

> We are not arguing against medical progress, for a great deal of useful knowledge is potentially available through *in vitro* research. We are simply concerned that Americans spell out carefully what progress means before they endorse it.[100]

Having a child

Obviously a major implication of the practice of surrogacy is that a couple who wanted a child with some genetic link to themselves now have one. For the couple, this can be the fulfillment of their dreams of having a family, the end of a frustrating period of stress, tension, and disappointment. The family can now move into a new phase of development and live out its expectations.

For the surrogate, too, there are implications. She has given something to a couple that few others would. She has given them a joy almost beyond their beliefs and hopes. Additionally, the surrogate has the satisfaction of economic reward. While the surrogate and rearing family may both have personalized their service of the surrogate, nonetheless the service was performed under contract and there were expectations on the part of each. And for fulfilling her part of the contract, the surrogate is paid. She now returns to her life and can have a genuine sense of satisfaction.

Thus for these participants, the implications are typically positive. Each has received what he or she wanted and each now enjoys that. In spite of these genuine positive implications, some other issues need to be considered.

Family issues

There are issues affecting the family of the surrogate. If, for example, the surrogate has other children, can the practice of surrogacy threaten the parent-child relation? To put it bluntly, will the children of the surrogate's family wonder if they too might be given away or sold? Since it is desirable that surrogates have had prior children, that issue is important. So far there have been no reports of this happening. But then too, the families of surrogates have not been studied. Similarly, might not the husband of the surrogate also be vulnerable to developing negative feelings toward his wife.? She is pregnant with another man's child, and even though this was done artifically, the developing pregnancy is a constant reminder of the extramarital origin of the pregnancy. Even in the best of circumstances, that is, when the insemination is consented to by all parties and the pregnancy is a totally positive experience, the relationship of husband and wife also undergoes a new development as a consequence of the pregnancy and some strains in the relationship are likely. These tend, typically, to be resolved through growing into the new role of parenthood. These same issues may arise during a surrogate pregnancy but may not be attended to or resolved because the baby will not stay in the family. Thus there may be many unresolved developmental issues surrounding the pregnancy. These may be augmented by the depression that sometimes follows birth or by mourning that may accompany the surrender of the child.

It is unclear whether these or other developmental issues may accompany the surrogate pregnancy and birth. The issues are significant, however, and they should be considered. It would be a relief to know these problems are only hypothetical. It would be a tragedy to assume they will not happen and then have a family harmed by the practice of surrogacy.

Another problem can arise from the asymmetry of the relation to the child by the adopting/rearing family.[101] The child has a genetic relation to the father. Can this cause difficulties in the bonding process, the relation of the spouses to each other, and in child-rearing practices? Will the unequal biological relation cause long-term problems? Such asymmetrical relations have caused problems in the blended families of second marriages. Even though the surrogacy arrangement may not necessarily complicate parent-child relations with the trauma of a divorce, the asymmetry is there.

Consider, for example, a couple which received a child from a surrogate. The couple divorces after several years. The custody of the child could be problematic. The child clearly has a biological relation to the father. Should this take priority over the mother's claims of a moral relation and perhaps a relation coming from legal adoption? Or can the biological relation take precedence over the father's desire not to have custody? Here the father would be required to take custody. Again no cases have been presented, but given divorce statistics, one is sure to present itself and significant custody issues will be raised.

Disposition of the child

Another set of issues is raised by competing claims about the disposition of the child. One set of issues is raised when the adopting/rearing family does not want the child to which the surrogate has given birth and the other occurs when the surrogate chooses not to surrender the child after birth. Examples of each have been reported in the media.

In one highly publicized and controversial case, in which many facts of the case were learned on the *Donahue* television show, the biological/rearing father refused to accept the child because of the possibility of retardation.[102] The surrogate also refused to accept the baby. On the *Donahue* show it was announced that the baby's genetic makeup differed from the biological/rearing father and in fact was the child of the surrogate and her husband. Evidently they had unprotected intercourse before insemination and she was already pregnant. Eventually the "surrogate" and her husband accepted the baby.

While the mode in which this situation was handled was particularly tasteless, the problem is a real one. While present contracts say nothing about the health of the baby as a condition for adoption, there is in principle nothing preventing a couple from insisting on that as a condition of acceptance of the baby. The problem then is what to do with the baby. Since the surrogate undertook the pregnancy precisely to deliver the baby to another, it is relatively obvious that she does not want the baby. And since the genetic/adopting parents have specified the type of baby they want, it is clear that they want only a certain kind of child. But here is a baby. One can safely predict additional problems for the child if one or the other is forced to accept it. Yet what is to be its fate? The baby did not ask to be born and is not responsible for its condition. Yet it is now unwanted. The problem is clear, but the solution is not.

The other issue, one with some precedents, is that of the surrogate's keeping the baby in spite of a contract to turn over the child to the biological father. While this issue has been resolved informally in past cases,[103] a contemporary case may set a precedent for future cases.[104] Mary Beth Whitehead agreed to be a surrogate and turn the baby over to the the couple after birth. But she became emotionally attached to the child, a girl referred to as Baby M, and refused to relinquish her to the adopting parents.[105] After two long and bitter trials, the baby was awarded to the contracting couple.

The child is the biological product of a male and female related only by a surrogacy contract which specifies that the biological mother will surrender the child after birth. The case complicated the lives of the surrogate, her husband and their two children, the biological father and his wife, and, of course, the child. Both parties have a traditional claim on the child: a biological relation. But they have no claim on each other other than a contractual one. At issue is the status of that contract and how one will decide the destiny of a child with two unrelated biological parents, both of whom claim the child.

The child will be surrounded by an atmosphere of controversy and possible hostility even after the appeal process is completed. For she will be a constant reminder of the conflict surrounding her conception, birth, and placement. Even though she may be given the best of affection, an atmosphere of controversy will surround her. Such an environment is not the best for anyone. Yet if the practice of surrogacy increases, such conflicts may become more and more common.

Eugenic concerns

The development of various reproductive technologies combined with the use of surrogates has reraised eugenic concerns. Given IVF, the capacity to examine, freeze, and successfully thaw embryos, various intrauterine monitoring technologies such as amniocentesis, fetoscopy, ultrasound, and other diagnostic means, we have the capacity to monitor the embryo at almost every stage of its existence and intervene at various stages of development. Surrogates themselves also are frequently selected on the basis of their physical appearance, physical and mental health, and IQ. Thus the door is open in a radically new way for the design and selection of our descendants.[106]

While the eugenic concerns focus mainly on technological means to achieve a certain end, surrogacy has a place as an alternative means through which designed and selected children can be born. There is in fact a strong hint of implicit eugenics in surrogacy contracts which require amniocentesis and mandate abortion if the embryo tests positive for selected traits. While this is but an extension of current practice in obstetrics, the eugenic direction is there.

Concern for the genetic health of a child raises critical moral issues. If such diseases can be prevented and are not, we would judge that as morally reprehensible. But eliminating the disease by eliminating the patient is surely a strange way to practice medicine. Designing a human to meet specific criteria raises other ethical issues as well with respect to the limits on our moral ability to intervene in the human genotype. In itself surrogacy is not an inherent part of the eugenics package. Nonetheless its practice is another component in a system that aims to redefine the nature of being human. One should, therefore, not condemn surrogacy as the next logical step in a eugenics program. But neither should one see it in isolation from such an orientation.

Feminist issues

Concerns about surrogacy are also raised from feminist perspectives. Andrea Dworkin, for example, speaks of a transition from the traditional brothel to a reproductive brothel. In the traditional brothel sex without reproduction is sold; in the reproductive brothel reproduction without sex is sold.[107] Dworkin argues that the same reasoning used to justify organized prostitution will be used to justify surrogacy. How can the state interfere in a woman's exercise of freedom? How can the state deny a woman the right to exercise her femininity through selling/renting her reproductive capacity? How can the state justify prohibiting a woman from participating in our free market system?

> In the new prostitution of reproduction, which is just beginning to unfold, the third party that will develop the female population for sale will be the scientist or doctor. He is a new kind of pimp, but he is not a new enemy of women. The formidable institutions of scientific research institutes and medical hospitals will be the new house out of which women are sold to men: the use of their wombs for money.[108]

Even if one discounts the harshness of the critique, one cannot avoid admitting that Dworkin has a solid point. Surrogates are typically chosen from a photo album which also lists their characteristics. They are paid for their services. They are expected to disappear when the service is finished. Both are valued for and reduced to only one aspect of their sexuality. There are differences, however, between a surrogate and a prostitute: the surrogate is expected to become pregnant and a prostitute is not: and intercourse for a surrogate is with a syringe, whereas with a prostitute both biological and technical means are used.

The comparison between surrogates and prostitutes is a harsh one. Nonetheless, points of contact are there and a major concern with the institutionalization of surrogacy is what it says about the role of women in society, especially with respect to their reduction to sexual parts and their being bought, sold, or rented.

Gena Corea also argues that the reproductive technologies are transforming women's reproductive experience by masculinizing it. She argues that for the male, reproduction is a discontinuous experience in that after insemination he is not directly or biologically involved in the growth of the fetus. For the woman, however, the experience of reproduction only begins at fertilization. The fertilized egg grows in her for nine months and the pregnancy is a part of her daily physical and psychological reality. The pregnancy is bodily present to her in a way inaccessible to a male and this somatic reality shapes her experiences in a much different way.[109]

The birth technologies, and surrogate motherhood in particular, transform the experience of pregnancy. Because in surrogacy the pregnancy is removed from the mother, even if she is the egg donor, her experience of pregnancy is also discontinuous. Her claim to maternity is made more distant, while the male's is advanced. She must now reconceptualize pregnancy and redetermine her contribution to it.

> Through her egg? Through her womb? Through her labor? As paternity always has been, maternity is becoming an act of intellect—for example, making a causal connection between the extraction of an egg and the birth of a child to another woman nine months later.[110]

By locating pregnancy or the components of a pregnancy in different individuals, the experience of pregnancy will change radically. It will be more externalized, more abstract, more rationalized, and more professionalized. Further, as many individuals as have had a role in the fertilization process will have a biological claim on the fetus. This will complicate understandings of parenthood, determination of lineage, and family relations, and will transform reproduction into a technique.

Some may argue, however, that this is all the better for women for now they are at last free. Their anatomy is no longer their destiny. Like men they can be present only at the inception of conception and then be free to to go about their business. No longer will they be restricted by their biology, by dysfunctional consequences of pregnancy. Assuredly so, but one must ask if such freedom is worth the price. The consequence of stereotypical male involvement in pregnancy may have led to less involvement with the pregnancy, less bonding, less appreciation of the mystery of life that is unfolding. Without romanticizing pregnancy, it puts one in touch with life and overcomes many of our routine alienations.

Freedom seldom comes without a price as many in the women's movement are discovering. The consequences of introducing such discontinuities into the critical and very personal experience of reproduction must be carefully considered.

How women relate to reproduction is clearly a function of their socialization, the role models they have experienced, and the various ideologies to which they consciously or unconsciously subscribe. The technologies available to us also help shape our social consciousness and our relations to self and others. The reproductive technologies give us new powers over reproduction; to experience the use and consequences of those capacities will help transform our understanding of reproduction and parenthood. In customary reproduction, it is possible to experience an organic relation to reproduction. The new technologies may succeed in breaking that relation by rationalizing it. This will then affect the status, perception, and role of women. While the possibility of liberation from biology is surely present in these technologies, they also contain the potential for a continued imprisonment of women in their traditional roles as breeders and of distancing them from their own bodies.

CONCLUSION

This chapter has considered a variety of ethical perspectives and problems related to the practice of surrogacy. Some of these issues are speculative, others are already being experienced. It is clear that the practice of surrogacy will bring tremendous changes to the personal and social experience of parenthood, fatherhood, and motherhood.

We have developed rather straightforwardly from the introduction of effective contraceptives which separated reproduction from intercourse to the birth technologies which separate reproduction from any expression of sexuality. The experience of conception has been rationalized and put in a clinical context. The reproductive process can be divided up between as many as five different individuals (or more if one includes the staff), all of whom can be a direct participant in the pregnancy and birth experience. To provide this form of reproduction is not simply to provide another "option" for those wanting a child. It is to transform our social and personal understanding of pregnancy, parenthood, and the family. That such institutions should not be changed or developed is not the issue. That we should be conscious of and responsible for the changes we introduce through technology is the issue and the point to which these ethical concerns are addressed.

To introduce a technology that will have profound effects on major and elementary social institutions without considering or studying them is, in my judgment, irresponsible. At present some deny that there will be any problems, others apparently do not worry about them, and others are raising concerns. We have a history of technology which alerts us to the myriad of social transformations occurring in the wake of technological interventions.

Yet we live in a culture which celebrates freedom and privacy and resists strongly any interferences into lifestyle options. Major battles have been fought and won to ensure that the state or others may not interfere with the acts of consenting adults. Thus many strongly resist any interference or hint of it. And their point is well taken.

However we do not exist as isolated individuals. Even our private acts have social implications or consequences. And this is particularly true of acts surrounding pregnancy. The birth technologies have the capacity to contribute to redefinitions of the family, parenthood, motherhood, fatherhood, the relation of a child to those responsible for his or her creation, and the other social institutions surrounding the family. Thus the ethical and social implications are significant, and we must weigh various values as we continue to think through how best to deal with these technologies and their profound consequences.

Part of this is being accomplished through the development of legislation or guidelines which regulate these technologies. We now turn to an examination of these statutes as the final element in our investigation of surrogacy before we begin drawing conclusions.

·5·

The Regulation
of Surrogate Motherhood

Given the various controversies about and implications of surrogate motherhood, it is no wonder that the question of regulation has been raised.[1] Although many are loathe to regulate what can be defined as a private practice or a medical decision, the social complexities are such that at least some discussions of regulations must begin.[2]

The primary motivation for these discussions was the Australian case of the orphaned embryos. In 1981 Mario and Elsa Rios, who were attempting in vitro fertilization, asked that the remaining embryos be frozen for use in later attempts at fertilization. The couple died in a plane crash in 1984. Since they had made no provision for the disposition of the embryos, an international debate arose about their fate. This debate was complicated by the fact that the embryos stood to inherit the large estate of their parents and by the later discovery that Mr. Rios was not the sperm donor. Although a committee eventually decided that the embryos should be removed from storage and allowed to expire, the issue was far from resolved.[3]

Because of the social implications of surrogacy and the increasing number of births by surrogates—now estimated to be around five hundred—several approaches to its regulation were initiated in various ways in different countries. Frequently these regulations are addressed to the broader issue of technical or noncoital reproduction and treat surrogacy within this context. This chapter will present an overview of what these policies or regulations have to say about surrogacy only.[4]

124

INTERNATIONAL PERSPECTIVES

Australia

Since much of the work on artificial reproduction occurs in Australia, it is fitting that this country has taken the lead in the articulation of guidelines.

In September 1982 the National Health and Medical Research Council of Australia issued a supplementary note to their *Statement on Human Experimentation*. This statement defined IVF and embryo transfer (ET) as acceptable means of treating infertility and determined that, even though they are established procedures, further research needs to be done. While the guidelines assume that IVF and ET will normally use sperm and ova from the partners, they recognize that at times ova from a donor may be necessary. The following regulations guide that donation.

> (a) the transfer would be part of the treatment within an accepted family relationship;
> (b) the recipient couple should intend to accept the duties and obligations of parenthood;
> (c) consent should be obtained from the donor and the recipient couple;
> (d) there should be no element of commerce between the donor and recipient couple;
> 4. A woman could produce a child for an infertile couple from ova and sperm derived from that couple. Because of current inability to determine or define motherhood in this context, this situation is not yet capable of ethical resolution.[5]

These regulations certainly recognize many of the difficulties in the situation of artificial reproduction but provide only general guidelines for regulating it. Of interest is the regulation's reticence about the practice of surrogacy. The regulations do not prohibit the practice. They simply recognize that as yet the practice is incapable of ethical resolution. Whether this lack of ethical resolution is enough to prohibit the practice is not stated. One may, evidently, infer what conclusion one wants.

Such ambiguity was resolved in the September 1982 *Interim Report* of the Victorian government committee established to deal with these issues. This report identified a number of issues related to IVF and ET which need resolution, including surrogate motherhood and the possibility of a totally extrauterine pregnancy. The recommendations, however, focused primarily on IVF and stated that "the IVF programme be limited to cases in which the gametes are obtained from husband and wife and the embryos are transferred into the uterus of the wife."[6] This effectively eliminates the possibility of surrogacy as part of the infertility program.

Further clarification came in the *Report on the Disposition of Embryos Produced by In Vitro Fertilization* (August 1984). This report was issued by the Victorian government committee to consider social, ethical, and legal issues arising from IVF. Essentially, it validates the donation of both egg and sperm to be used in IVF programs, as well as the development and maintenance of a cryopreservation program. Within this context, the commission makes several recommendations.

> 6.7 The couple whose gametes are used may not sell or casually dispose of the embryo.
>
> 6.17 A hospital licensed to conduct an IVF programme shall not be permitted to make any commercial surrogacy arrangements as part of that program.
>
> 6.18 Surrogacy arrangements shall in no circumstances be made at present as part of an IVF programme.[7]

The regulations clearly prohibit the selling and casual disposal of embryos. They also appear to prohibit coupling a surrogacy program with an IVF program. But they do not appear to prohibit surrogacy per se.

The intent of the regulations is to establish procedures for the appropriate disposition of gametes and embryos. Thus surrogacy is discussed indirectly and only in terms of commercialization as an inappropriate means of disposing of embryos. Volunteer or donor surrogacy may be permissible according to these guidelines.

The Australian guidelines express caution concerning surrogacy, for example, by prohibiting any linking of IVF programs and surrogacy. There is a consistent ban on the commercialization of surrogacy. And there is a recognition of the social, ethical, and legal difficulties surrounding the program. But this has not led the various provinces to prohibit surrogacy. Thus surrogates are used to resolve infertility, but its development is independent of the research and development programs in IVF.

The United Kingdom

England is the home of the first child born of in vitro fertilization, and thus it is natural that there would be guidelines to examine various aspects of the birth technologies. These deliberations began in 1978 and examined specifically IVF and embryo transfer in humans. The initial research was allowed to continue and was defined as a therapeutic procedure.[8] Again in 1982 the Medical Research Council reviewed developments and concluded:

> Scientifically sound research involving experiments on the processes and products of in vitro fertilisation between human gametes is ethically acceptable and should be allowed to proceed on condition both that there is no intent to transfer to the uterus any embryo resulting from or used in such experiments and also that the aim of the research is clearly defined and directly relevant to clinical problems such as contraception or the differential diagnosis and treatment of infertility and inherited diseases.[9]

In May 1982 the British Medical Association established a working group which issued the 1982 *Interim Report on Human In Vitro Fertilisation and Embryo Replacement and Transfer*. In typical British understatement, the working group concluded that it

> had yet to be satisfied that to undertake in vitro fertilisation with the sperm and the ova of a couple and to transfer the embryo to the uterus of another woman who might carry the embryo to term on behalf of the couple will ever be acceptable.[10]

However, even in England practice soon outstripped expectations or even acceptability. In 1984 another committee was formed under the leadership of Dame Mary Warnock to reexamine the ethical, legal, and social dilemmas associated with artificial reproduction. Their recommendations on surrogacy are particularly interesting in that the report places a total ban on surrogacy. However, there is a minority dissent which suggests a small, controlled opening.

After reviewing the arguments for surrogacy[11] (an act of generosity, the possession of a right to use one's body as one wants, and surrogacy's being the only chance for a child genetically related to at least one partner) and the reasons against it (negative public opinion, the introduction of a third party into the marital relation, inconsistent with human dignity to treat a woman as an incubator, and negative consequences on the child and parental relationship), the committee made these two major recommendations.

> 8.18. We recommend that legislation be introduced to render criminal the creation or the operation in the United Kingdom of agencies whose purposes include the recruitment of women for surrogate pregnancy or making arrangments for individuals or couples who wish to utilise the services of a carrying mother; such legislation should be wide enough to include both profit and non-profit making organisations. We further recommend that the legislation be sufficiently wide to render criminally liable the actions of professionals and others who knowingly assist in the establishment of a surrogate pregnancy.
> 8.19 We recommend that it be provided by statute that all surrogacy agreements are illegal contracts and therefore unenforceable in the courts.[12]

Such recommendations clearly remove any legal sanctioning for structures supporting the establishment of surrogacy. No one can set himself or herself up as the "matchmaker" between potential surrogates and a couple. No professional may assist in establishing such a pregnancy and any contracts entered into are illegal. The recommendations remove the social sanctioning necessary for surrogacy and made it illegal. And while the recommendations cannot control what goes on in a private lab or what individuals may choose to do on their own, such practices are not sanctioned and no legal recourse is available in the event of a problem.

Nonetheless, two members of the committee recognize that the demand for surrogacy will continue to grow, especially on the part of those who have no other opportunity to have a child related genetically to at least one of the partners. Such couples may be driven into very risky situations to obtain their child. Also the two dissenters were concerned with the outcomes of surrogacy: Will the public accept it? Are the consequences acceptable or not? What might the demand be? A total prohibition, as proposed in the majority report, will not be able to respond to these issues.

Therefore these two members recommend that a Licensing Authority "have the power to license an agency or agencies to make arrangements for surrogacy."[13] This agency would match surrogates with parents, provide counseling, and have no commercial interest. All other surrogacy arrangements would come under the ban proposed by the majority. Additionally, these commissioners recognize that since most surrogates expect some payment, that "should not be a barrier to the child being adopted by the commissioning parents."[14]

Thus, while liberal on the use of IVF as a method of treating infertility,[15] the Warnock Commission is very conservative on the issue of surrogacy. And since it is not sanctioned, no means are available to determine whether the assumed negative consequences on the basis of which the practice was prohibited will actually occur.

THE UNITED STATES

In rather typical fashion, the technologies of artificial reproduction have developed in advance of any legal, social, or ethical analysis. The American practice is to let a particular technology go forward and to examine it only after it is established. While providing the advantage of allowing an examination of actual consequences, the procedure is as effective as locking the proverbial barn door after the horse has escaped.

Yet some context is available in the United States for the policy evaluation of surrogacy. This consists of federal regulations, state laws, court cases, and the recommendations of professional societies.

Federal Regulations: The Ethics Advisory Board

The Ethics Advisory Board (EAB) was commissioned to examine the specific question of whether or not the Department of Health and Human Services (HHS) should fund studies on IVF and embryo transfer. Thus the EAB did not, nor was it expected to, consider the question of surrogacy. But its conclusions had an impact on surrogacy.

Two questions under consideration by the EAB concerned the ethics of research on IVF and embryo transfer and the question of funding. Thus the issues are narrowly drawn, but the conclusions are fairly general.

> (1) The Department should consider support of more animal research in order to assess the risks to both mother and offspring associated with the procedures; (2) the conduct of research involving human *in vitro* fertilization designed to establish the safety and effectiveness of the procedure is ethically acceptable under certain conditions; (3) Departmental support of such research would be acceptable from an ethical standpoint, although the Board did not address the question of the level of funding, if any, which such research might be given; (4) the Department should take the initiative in collecting, analyzing and disseminating data from both research and clinical practice involving *in vitro* fertilization throughout the world; and (5) model or uniform laws should be developed to define the rights and responsibilities of all parties involved in such activities.[16]

The immediate effect of these recommendations was to remove the federal government from any influence on this area. Since no reviewing agency for protocols was established, no funding was made available, and no laws were in place (which is what the commission recommended making), the funding of research and development shifted to the private sector. Consequently, the traditional beginning of research with the developmental of animal models and limited human trials was almost bypassed in favor of immediate clinical applications.

By deciding not to fund research on IVF and other means of artificial reproduction, the federal government lost any control that it might have desired to have. If HHS funded any research, the investigators would be subject to any constraints HHS would have instituted. As it is, the only restraints are the adequacy of the money to carry out a project and the personal ethical standards of the practitioner.

State Laws

While at present only Kentucky has a court decision specificially permitting surrogates to be paid and the New Jersey Supreme Court has denied the validity of the surrogacy contract, the laws of many other states have an indirect bearing on surrogacy.[17] For example, many states regulate research on human fetuses. IVF, embryo transfer, or one of the other birth technologies could be construed as a form of research and thus fall under this prohibition. Massachusetts, for example, has fairly restrictive legislation governing fetal research. Since this legislation was passed prior to the development of the reproductive technologies, it is unclear how it might apply to them.[18] Other states have laws governing artificial insemination. Thus should a man donate sperm to inseminate a woman not his wife, the donor is not the father of the child.[19] Such legislation protects sperm donors from being sued for support. Other state laws make the husband of the woman artificially inseminated the father if he consented. This presents a legal challenge to the claims of the rearing couple, even though the male of this couple donated the sperm.[20] Some states prohibit payment in connection with an adoption and this may complicate the issue of the payment of a surrogate. Additionally, other states prohibit the donation and/or selling of an embryo or fetus either in general or for research purposes.

State laws can indirectly complicate the practice of surrogacy while not directly impinging on the issue. Especially critical are the laws concerning artificial insemination by donor (AID). AID is a relatively common practice to resolve infertility and laws were enacted to ensure the legitimacy of the child or to establish paternity. But while having these important social functions, these laws completely undercut the claim to paternity of the rearing father who is also the sperm donor. For although biologically the father, the sperm donor is not the legal father. However, it is the claim of biological fatherhood that invalidates the necessity of the donor's legally adopting the child to become its father. Thus the AID laws can create a situation in which the biological father cannot be the legal father and in which a consenting husband becomes a legal father even though he wants nothing to do with the child or process.

As laws are developed, great care will have to be taken to coordinate existing laws so that unfortunate complications do not arise and the last condition is worse than the first.

Court Cases

As should have been expected, a number of surrogate cases have wound up in court. However, only a few have actually gone to trial. Out-of-court settlements have resolved the issue for other cases. Thus on a few court cases directly related to surrogacy are available.

A court-determined right to reproduce stands as the generic background to all surrogate cases. This was established first in *Skinner* v. *Oklahoma*[21] which affirmed a right to reproduce in opposition to a state initiative to sterilize habitual criminals. This was followed by *Griswold* v. *Connecticut*[22] which affirmed a right to use contraceptives based on a concept of marital privacy. Similar to this was *Eisenstadt* v. *Baird*[23] which prohibited the banning of contraceptives. In *Carey* v. *Population Services International*, the Supreme Court overrode a New York State court by arguing that the "decision whether or not to beget or bear a child [is] . . . at the very heart of [the] cluster of constitutionally protected choices."[24] Finally, *Roe* v. *Wade*[25] determined that the right of privacy was broad enough to encompass a woman's decision whether or not to terminate her pregnancy.

While not related directly to the issue of surrogacy, the establishment of the right to certain freedoms and privacy surrounding reproduction provides a point of departure for some of the surrogacy issues. Of particular concern in future decisions will be how a general reproductive right will interact with legislation prohibiting the exchange of money in an adoption procedure or whether a reproductive right also establishes a right to use or demand access to particular technologies. For example, the Illinois case of *Willey* v. *Lawton*[26] held as unenforceable an agreement between the birth parents and the adopting parents to pay for the adoption of the child. On the other hand, the case *In re Estate of Shirk*[27] permitted a family compact in which the natural mother consented to the grandmother's adoption of her child in return for which the mother and child would share in the grandmother's estate upon the death of the grandmother. This decision did not seem counter to public policy against selling or bartering children because it attempted to seek the best interests of the child. Additionally, the child remained within the context of the biological family. Thus, when the practice of surrogacy is advanced in court, several critical issues will be joined.

Doe, Roe, et al. v. Kelley and Cahalan[28]

This is the first of a series of cases dealing with the issue of whether or not a surrogate can be paid for her services. The plaintiffs contested sections of the Michigan adoption laws which prohibited the exchange of money or other valuable considerations in an adoption proceeding. They also argued that such an arrangement on their part is constitutionally protected under the provisions for privacy.

The plaintiffs contended that the appropriate Michigan law was too vague with respect to specification of payment and that, therefore, it was void. The court argued, first, that "the statute in the instant case is as specific is as [sic] necessary to give fair notice to those to whom the statute is directed,"[29] and, second, that "it is not necessary that the statute list all conceivable items of value to be constitutionally specific."[30] Thus the law need not explicitly mention payment to a surrogate to be relevant to the instant case.

The privacy issue is the more substantive one and the court responded at length. Beginning with the assumption of privacy and its relevance to procreation, contraception, and family issues, the court nonetheless argued that the right is "specific, narrow and is not of the same personal nature that the constitutional right of privacy protects."[31] Thus the court concluded:

> It is this Court's opinion that a contract to use the statutory authority of the Probate Court to effect the *adoption* of a child

> wherein such contract provides for valuable compensation, is
> not deserving of, nor is it within the constitutional protection
> of the right of privacy as defined by the many cases of the
> United States Supreme Court.[32]

Then the court proceeded to provide other arguments whichit thought would overcome a right to privacy if such a right shouldbe applicable. First, the right is not absolute and can be overridden by important state interests. These include, but are not limited to, the prevention of commercialism from affecting a mother's decision to adopt, prohibiting "baby bartering," andpreventing harm to the family that could come from introducingcommercialism into it.[33] Second, the court argued that the legislation in question is sufficiently narrowly drawn so as to expressthe legitimate interest of the state.

Thus in this first case the adopting parents were not able toenter a contract to pay the surrogate a fee over and beyond hermedical and health related expenses.

Syrkowski v. *Appleyard*[34]

This case sought an "order of filiation and entry of petitioner'sname on the birth certificate as natural and legal father of a childto be born to a surrogate mother."[35] The plaintiff also attemptedto broaden the terms of the Paternity Act to encompass the feepaid to a surrogate.

The court essentially argued that "Statutes are to be construedas they were intended to be understood when they were passed."[36]On that basis, the court concluded that reading the PaternityAct, whose primary purpose was to provide support for childrenborn out of wedlock, "does not encompass the monetary transaction proposed in the case."[37] Thus even though all partiesagreed to the facts of the case—the woman was artificially inseminated with the plaintiff's semen, her husband surrenderedany claim to paternity, and the plaintiff wished to have his nameon the birth certificate as the natural father—the court disallowedthe payment of a fee to the surrogate.

Subsequently, legislation was introduced in Michigan to permitthe practice of surrogacy, including the paying of a fee to thesurrogate, but this legislation has not passed as of this writing.

Doe v. *Kelly*[38]

Michigan law prohibits, in adoption procedures, any payment of consideration beyond court approved expenses. The plaintiffs petitioned to have such a provision declared unconstitutional because it was an impermissible intrusion into their rights of privacy. The court argued that the law did not prohibit the couple from having the surrogacy arrangement. Rather,

> It acts instead to preclude plaintiffs from paying consideration in conjunction with their use of the state's adoption procedures. In effect, the plaintiff's contractual agreement discloses a desire to use the adoption code to change the legal status of the child—i.e., its right to support, intestate succession, etc. We do not perceive this goal as within the realm of fundamental interests protected by the right to privacy from reasonable governmental regulation.[39]

The issue is not a constitutionally protected right to bear a child; it is payment to the surrogate. The court concluded that such a practice exceeded the limits of the regulations surrounding adoption.

Surrogate Parenting Associates v. *Commonwealth of Kentucky*[40]

This Kentucky case claims that surrogate parenthood contracts violate three aspects of its adoption statutes: (1) the law prohibits the procurement or sale of a child for adoption; (2) the prohibition for filing a petition to the voluntary termination of parental rights "prior to five (5) days after the birth of a child"; and (3) consent for adoption is not valid if given prior to the fifth day after the birth of a child.[41]

The issues of the case center around whether or not a surrogate may be paid a fee for her services. This was the third hearing of this case. A circuit court previously held that the Surrogate Parenting Associates (SPA) activities were not illegal. A court of appeals reversed this decision. Then, before this Kentucky Supreme Court hearing, the legislature revised a statute of the adoption legislation to prohibit:

> the purchase of any child for the purpose of adoption or any other purpose, including termination of parental rights.[42]

The question the state supreme court set out to answer is "whether SPA's involvement in the surrogate parenting procedure should be construed as participation in the buying and selling of babies as prohibited by KRS 199.590(2)."[43] Thus the issue is one of legislation, and the court saw itself as an interpreter of legislation and not a setter of public policy, a task for the legislature. The court concluded its hearing by saying:

> We agree with the trial court that if there is a judgment to be made outlawing such a procedure, it is a matter for the legislature. The surrogate parenting procedure as outlined in the Stipulation of Facts is not foreclosed by legislation now on the books. The judgment of the Court of Appeals is reversed. The judgment of the trial court is affirmed.[44]

Thus the decision cleared the way for the surrogate to be paid for her services. However, two of the justices dissented from this opinion. Justice Vance argued that since half of the surrogate's fee is paid only after the delivery of the baby and is accompanied by a quit-claim deed which terminates her parental rights, this constitutes the sale of a baby and thus violates the law. Justice Wintersheimer, agreeing with Justice Vance, also argued that such surrogate procedures open the way for the exploitation of women and are thus undesirable. Such practices also would violate a public interest in preserving the traditional family.

Thus the majority opinion argued the case on the issue of whether or not such a practice is specifically prohibited by current law. The majority determination was that it did not because the law prohibiting termination of parental rights does not extend to the surrogacy situation. The dissenting opinions, however, looked at the implications of the practices as well as the manner of the transfer of the child and concluded that the implications were serious enough to prohibit the practice.

*In the Matter of the Adoption
of Baby Girl, L. J., Anonymous*[45]

This New York case also focuses specifically on the issue of payment to the surrogate. After reviewing decisions by the Michigan and Kentucky courts, the New York court concluded:

Current legislation does not expressly forclose the use of surrogate mothers or the paying of compensation to them under parenting agreements. Accordingly, the court finds that this is a matter for the legislature to address rather than for the judiciary to attempt to determine by the impermissible means of "judicial" legislation. In its absence, this court will not appropriate the function of the legislature and prohibit such arrangements.[46]

Thus this court also finds no inherent conflict between the adoption statutes as written and the payment of fees to surrogates. However, this court also recognized the strong need for legislation in this area.

In the Matter of Baby "M," a pseudonym for an actual person[47]

This major surrogacy case pitted William and Elizabeth Stern against Mary Beth Whitehead over the custody of Baby M whom Mrs. Whitehead bore under contract for William Stern who is the biological father of the child. After the birth, Mrs. Whitehead decided to keep the child, thus setting off a bitter, protracted, and exhaustively reported battle.

Mary Beth Whitehead, a twenty-nine-year-old married woman with two children of that marriage, contracted with William and Elizabeth Stern to be artificially inseminated by Mr. Stern and to surrender her parental rights so that the Sterns could become the legal parents. The Sterns paid the Infertility Center of New York a ten-thousand-dollar nonrefundable fee and put ten thousand more in escrow with the center to pay the surrogate after she delivered the baby to them. The Sterns would further pay associated medical expenses which were estimated to be an additional five thousand dollars.[48]

After the birth of the baby, Mrs. Whitehead changed her mind and kept the baby, refused to take the ten thousand dollars and fled to Florida with her husband to avoid a New Jersey court order to turn over the baby to the Sterns. The Sterns initiated a suit to secure the specific performance of the contract, that is, to have her surrender the baby to them. The Sterns obtained court-ordered temporary custody of the baby, with Mrs. Whitehead having twice a week court-permitted visiting privileges.[49]

The Sterns have filed suit to gain full custody of the baby. And Mrs. Whitehead has filed a suit against the Infertility Center of New York claiming fraud, negligence, and breach of contract. Her intent is either to have the practice of surrogacy banned or to establish guidelines to safeguard women who contract to become surrogate mothers. After a very acrimonious trial, the judge decided in favor of the Sterns by upholding the validity of the contract. Mary Beth Whitehead lost her claim to the child, especially since the judge conducted an adoption procedure for Mrs. Stern immediately after he handed down his decision.

The two major issues examined by Judge Sorkow as the basis for his decision were the best interests of the child and the validity of the contract. Additionally, testimony was heard about the competence of each couple as parents. Such competence was a partial basis for deciding where the best interests of the child could be realized.

With respect to the contract, the judge found that there was no fraud or deception in its execution, that Mrs. Whitehead understood it, and that there was no coercion in signing it. Thus the contract is binding and its terms must be fulfilled. "There is no fraud, legal or equitable, that would allow Mr. and Mrs. Whitehead to recind their contract."[50] Thus the baby was turned over to the Sterns and all visitation rights by the Whiteheads were denied. Finally, immediately after the trial, Judge Sorkow took the Sterns into his chambers where Mrs. Stern legally adopted the baby.

The case raised all the worse possible scenarios with surrogacy: a surrogate who breeches a contract by refusing to surrender the baby; a custody dispute between two individuals who are the biological parents but are not related in any way; questioning the establishment, role, and status of surrogacy centers; how to proceed in the absence of guidelines. At the same time, the lives of the Whiteheads were subject to intense scrutiny.[51] The case is an important one because it brings together many of the issues that have been simmering for several years. It can set the precedents that could determine the future of surrogacy in this country.

In a similar case, the surrogate mother of twins has been awarded continued custody of them against the wishes of the biological father who contracted with this surrogate. He and his wife have two visits per week of one hour each; these are to be supervised by the court.[52] Additionally, other surrogates who have surrendered their children in accordance with the contract are banding together to seek the return of the children. Thus the cases that have come to court so far may represent the beginning of a reevaluation of surrogacy.

In the Matter of Baby M

On 4 February 1988 the Supreme Court of New Jersey announced the conclusions of its review of a lower court's decision in the Stern-Whitehead case. The lower court's judgment was affirmed in part, reversed in part, and remanded for further considerations.

What was reversed was critical: the surrogate contract was invalidated, the parental interests of the divorced and newly remarried Mary Beth Whitehead-Gould were restored, and the adoption invalidated. Affirmed was the Sterns' permanent custody.

> We invalidate the surrogacy contract because it conflicts with the law and public policy of this State. While we recognize the depth of the yearning of infertile couples to have their own children, we find the payment of money to a "surrogate" mother illegal, perhaps criminal, and potentially degrading to women. Although in this case we grant custody to the natural father, the evidence having clearly proved such custody to be in the best interests of the infant, we void both the termination of the surrogate mother's parental rights and the adoption of the child by the wife/stepparent. We thus restore the "surrogate" as the mother of the child.[53]

Two elements of the decision are significant for the broader discussion of surrogacy. First is the issue of parental rights. The court argued that the surrogacy contract violated state policy that "the rights of natural parents are equal concerning their child, the father's right no greater that the mother's."[54] This meant, for the court, that the "purpose and effect of the surrogacy contract was to give the father the exclusive right to the child by destroying the rights of the mother."[55] Thus this right has to be asserted of both. As the court says:

To assert that Mr. Stern's right of procreation gives him the
right to the custody of Baby M would be to assert that Mrs.
Whitehead does *not* give up the right to the custody of Baby
M.[56]

The second element is the court's discussion of the commercial
aspects of surrogacy. As noted previously, proponents of surrogacy argue that the money is a reimbursement for services,
while opponents argue that it is baby selling. The court left no
doubt about its position:

Its [the contract] use of money for this purpose—and we have
no doubt whatsoever that the money is being paid to obtain
an adoption and not, as the Sterns argue, for the personal
services of Mary Beth Whitehead—is illegal and perhaps
criminal.[57]

The court also noted several evils—to use its word—which
promped the payment of money.

First, and perhaps most important, all parties concede that
it is unlikely that surrogacy will survive without money. De-
spite the alleged selfless motivation of surrogate mothers, if
there is no payment, there will be no surrogates, or very few.

Second, the use of money in adoptions does not *produce* the
problem—conception occurs, and usually the birth itself, before illicit funds are offered.

Third, with the law prohibiting the use of money in connection with adoptions, the built-in financial pressure of the
unwanted pregnancy and the consequent support obligation
do not lead the mother to the highest paying, ill-suited, adoptive parents. She is just as well off surrendering the child to
an approved agency. In surrogacy, the highest bidders will
presumably become the adoptive parents regardless of suit-
ability, so long as payment of money is permitted.

Fourth, the mother's consent to surrender her child in
adoptions is revocable, even after surrender of the child, unless it be to an approved agency.[58]

Thus the New Jersey Supreme Court brought to conclusion a
difficult, complex, and highly controversial case. Obviously this

is one decision in one state and sets no national precedent. Yet the New Jersey Supreme Court is an important one and its decisions in other cases[59] have been landmark ones which influenced other courts. But clearly, as a consequence of this decision, the practice of surrogacy has encountered a substantive obstacle.

Professional Guidelines

As the reproductive technologies have become institutionalized in various clinics around the world, professional societies have begun to draft guidelines. These guidelines are intended to set professional standards in the absence of legislation and social and professional criteria for establishing a reproductive clinic.

The American College of Obstetricians and Gynecologists

The American College of Obstetricians and Gynecologists (ACOG) issued a policy statement in 1983.[60] This statement, still in effect, identifies various pros and cons, similarities of surrogacy with artificial insemination by donor, raises several concerns about surrogacy, and then states its policy.

The policy statement raises several concerns. These include the depersonalization, to some extent, of reproduction, stress in the relation of the infertile couple, the potential for eugenic manipulation, the potential impact of the technologies on the children, and the anonymity of the various parties. Specifically in relation to surrogacy, ACOG identifies the physical implications of the pregnancy and the separation of the infant from the surrogate as risk factors which may not be comprehended until experienced. Additionally, it is unclear who should receive the medical information and participate in decisions regarding the welfare of the fetus and newborn. This issue is important with respect to the possible desire to regulate the behavior of the surrogate during pregnancy. Also the surrogate may change her mind and seek either an abortion of the fetus or custody of the newborn.[61] Finally, the surrogate may find herself having custody of the newborn because the other couple does not want it.

ACOG specifically raises concerns about using surrogacy for convenience and raises three problems: (1) an increase of depersonalization; (2) a risk that could be born by the couple is assigned to someone else; (3) a questioning of the dedication to parenthood of the couple contracting for the surrogate.

Given these concerns, ACOG has "significant reservations about this approach to parenthood"[62] It then makes the following recommendations.

I. Initiation of Surrogate Arrangements

A. When approached by a patient interested in surrogate motherhood, the physician should, as in all other aspects of medical care, be certain there is a full discussion of ethical and medical risks, benefits and alternatives. . . .

B. A physician may justifiably decline to participate in surrogate motherhood arrangements.

C. If a physician decides to become involved in a surrogate motherhood arrangement, he or she should follow these guidelines:

1. The physician should be assured that appropriate procedures are utilized to screen the contracting couple and the surrogate. Such screening may include appropriate fertility studies and genetic screening.

2. The physician should receive only the usual compensation for obstetric and gynecologic services. Referral fees and other arrangements for financial gain beyond the usual fees for medical services are inappropriate.

3. The physician should not participate in a surrogate program where the financial arrangements are likely to exploit any of the parties.

II. Care of Pregnant Surrogates

A. When a woman seeks medical care for an established pregnancy, regardless of the method of conception, she should be cared for as any other obstetric patient or referred to a qualified physician who will provide that care.

B. The surrogate mother should be considered the source of consent with respect to clinical intervention and management of the pregnancy. Confidentiality between the physician and patient should be maintained.

If other parties, such as the adoptive parents, are to play a role in decision making, the parameters should be clearly delineated, with the agreement of the patient.[63]

These policy statements can hardly be considered a ringing endorsement of the practice of surrogacy. Nonetheless they recognize its reality by leaving the decision of whether or not to participate in it up to the individual practitioner. However, ACOG does not encourage its members to initiate such practices and only with reluctance does it condone individual decisions to participate in it.

The American Fertility Society

The American Fertility Society (AFS) recently completed a lengthy study of the ethical dimension of the reproductive technologies. Its findings have been released in the report "Ethical Considerations of the New Reproductive Technologies."[64] Although this report covers, from medical, legal, and ethical perspectives, the full range of reproductive technologies, only the section on surrogacy will be considered here.[65]

1. Surrogate Gestational Mothers. The report first considers surrogate gestational mothers, that is, women who are not genetically related to the embryo but who receive the embryo and carry it to term. The reason for such a practice is the inability of one woman to provide the gestational component for reproduction. She may, for example, lack a uterus or have severe hypertension.

The report identifies several risks associated with this procedure. The first set of concerns center on the surrogate. Thus a surrogate will face the risks of pregnancy and childbirth without a commensurate benefit. A surrogate who is a friend or relative of the couple may be coerced into providing this service. The surrogate also may be psychologically harmed.

A second set of issues relates to the couple. They could be harmed if the surrogate decides to keep the child. And if the surrogate is a friend or relative, strains may be introduced into the marital relation.

The third set of concerns focus on the child. Here the report recognizes that the behavior of the surrogate during the pregnancy could raise critical issues. If the child learns of his or her origins, will the fact of having two such mothers be detrimental to its development and identity. This may be of particular concern if the surrogate is a friend or relative of the rearing mother.

Two additional difficult issues are raised by the report. First, there is a recognition of the possibility of exploiting the couple and/or surrogate by professionals who act as the middle persons or brokers. Second, is surrogacy proper if the motivation is purely social, rather than based on some medical indication? That is, if the rearing mother simply does not want to bear the pregnancy even though she is capable of so doing, is it ethical for her to ask another to bear her risks?[66]

The report then indicates several reasons for the use of the surrogate gestational mother. First is that this may simply be the only way a couple can have a child. Then, such a practice provides an opportunity for the child to exist and be reared by a family that really wants him or her. Third, the procedure offers the woman an opportunity to be altruistic by providing a benefit for another couple. Fourth, some women enjoy being pregnant and this would allow them to enjoy that experience. Finally, some surrogates apparently use this experience to help themselves psychologically be reliving a pregnancy in a satisfactory manner.[67]

In its recommendations, the report rejects the use of surrogate gestational mothers for nonmedical reasons, such as the convenience of the genetic mother. However, it does see a role for it in reproductive medicine. But surrogacy should be understood as a clinical experiment[68] and, if it is carried out, the following issues should be addressed:

> a. the psychological effects of the procedure on the surrogate gestational mother, the couple, and the resulting child
> b. the possibility of any bonding between the surrogate gestational mother and the fetus in utero
> c. the appropriate screening of the gestational mother and of the couple who provide the sperm and egg
> d. the likelihood that the surrogate gestational mother will exercise appropriate care during pregnancy.
> e. the effects of having the couple and the surrogate gestational mother meet or not meet

f. the effects on the surrogate gestational mother's own family of her participation in the process

g. the effects of disclosing or not disclosing the use of a surrogate gestational mother or her identity to the child

h. other issues that shed light on the effects of surrogate gestational motherhood on the welfare of the various persons involved and on society.[69]

Additionally, the report emphasizes the necessity of informed consent and the need to screen the candidate medically. It urges that the professionals involved receive only their customary fees and that there be "no finder's fees for participation in surrogate motherhood."[70] And, finally, the report expresses a preference that the surrogate not be paid beyond compensation for expenses and inconveniences, although it is recognized that sometimes payment will be necessary for it to occur.

2. Surrogate Mothers. This section of the report evaluates the "traditional" meaning of a surrogate mother: one who is artificially inseminated with the sperm of the genetic and rearing father and who delivers the child to his custody after birth. Ironically, even though this is the form of surrogacy most commonly practiced, it has not received much medical attention. The report argues that this is the case because the practice has developed in "an entrepreneurial setting, generally apart from medical institutions."[71]

There are three indications for the use of such a surrogate: first, a woman may be unable to provide either the gestational or genetic component for child bearing, that is, the woman has had a hysterectomy combined with removal of the ovaries. Second, the woman cannot provide the genetic component, for example, if she were to have a genetic disease or experienced premature menopause. Third, the woman is unable to gestate, perhaps because of severe hypertension or some uterine malformation.[72]

Several reservations are then expressed about the practice of surrogacy. Concern is expressed about the propriety of putting oneself at the risk of pregnancy to benefit another. Fear is expressed that the surrogate may be harmed by surrendering the child. Also the surrogate may find herself with the unintended custody of a child either because a paternity test shows that the child is not genetically related to the sperm donor or because the sperm donor refuses to accept the child.

The couple may also be harmed or put at risk by not learning of alternative resolutions to infertility, by having the surrogate harass them after the birth of the child, or the couple may experience tension in their marriage because of continual involvement of the surrogate. Finally, the uncertain legal status of the procedure may cause anxiety and discomfort.

Several concerns about the effect of surrogacy on the child are also noted. The child could be harmed if the surrogate is not screened and consequently passes a genetic disease to him or her. Also, if the surrogate knows she will not rear the child, she may not be as concerned about its prenatal care or may give priority to herself in potential cases of conflict between herself and the fetus. Additionally, what impact will the knowledge of his or her origins have on the child's development? And if the surrogate maintains contact with the family, will the child be harmed by the presence of two mothers?

Three additional concerns are expressed. First is the impact of surrogacy on the stability of the family: Will third-party reproduction threaten the marital relation? Second, will payment of surrogates lead to the commercialization of reproduction, with children being seen as consumer items? And third, will a surrogate be used only for convenience?

Several benefits are identified with surrogacy. For the infertile wife the opportunity is there to adopt a child more quickly than the normal adoption process would allow, and she can help raise her husband's genetic child. For the husband a surrogate may be the "only way in which he can conceive and rear a child with a biologic tie to himself, short of divorcing his wife and remarrying only for that reason or of having an adulterous union."[73] And as benefit to the child, the use of a surrogate allows him or her to exist and be raised by a couple which deeply desires a child. The surrogate has an opportunity to perform an act of altruism, to repeat her enjoyment of pregnancy, to provide income for her family while remaining at home with other children, and to resolve issues from past pregnancies.[74]

In summary, then, the three areas of concern identified in the report are first, the previously mentioned risks for the surrogate, couple, and child; second, issues having to do with the potential for the commercialization of the process, especially since a set of brokers has arisen to help in the process; third, the lack of laws protecting all the parties involved.

Given this orientation, the report does not recommend the use of a surrogate for nonmedical reasons because such reasons do not appear to justify the risks of pregnancy and delivery. And although the writers of the report are concerned about the lack of knowledge of the surrogacy process and its effects, they recognize that it offers the "only medical solution to infertility in a couple of whom the woman has no uterus and who does not produce eggs or does not want to risk passing on a genetic defect that she carries."[75] The report does not recommend the widespread clinical application of surrogate motherhood but does not think there are adequate reasons to recommend legal prohibition. Thus, if pursued, surrogacy should be considered a clinical experiment and conducted with attention to the same set of questions and caveats quoted in the previous section.

The Ethics Committee of the American Fertility Society thus opposes the use of surrogate gestational mothers for medical reasons and is not favorably disposed to the use of surrogate mothers for medical reasons. Both should be considered clinical experiments and their consequences should be studied. Surrogate gestational motherhood can play a part in reproductive medicine, but its general application is premature. And while there appear to be no adequate reasons to recommend legal prohibition of surrogate motherhood, the committee has serious ethical reservations about it and these will not be resolved until further data are available. Thus it too should be considered a clinical experiment and general application should be considered as premature.

SUMMARY

This overview of regulatory activities reveals a wide range of perspectives on surrogacy. In general, one can note that there is an undercurrent of discomfort with—if not disapproval of—surrogacy. On the other hand, the level of disapproval is not such that surrogacy is to be totally banned, except in England where the establishment of surrogacy clinics and participation of professionals in surrogacy activities are to be made criminal. In Australia the tendency seems to be to split off the surrogacy arrangements from IVF clinics. And in America surrogacy is seen as problematic but having some merit for a certain class of problems. Thus one has the sense of an acceptance of the practice, but one which is given reluctantly.

The most significant regulatory problems will emerge from the various suits that will be brought as more and more people use surrogacy. This will happen because few state laws deal with surrogacy and people will use existing legislation to test its practice. Thus science is once again in front of law and ethics and the game is catch up. Additionally, the game is also being played under a set of practices that are being developed by various surrogate brokers. This means that practice is developing outside of the traditional observation of professionals in the field, Institutional Review Boards which review research on human subjects, and the restraints imposed by public funding agencies.

Obviously the practice of surrogacy is going forward. The questions are: How fast and how far? But until there is either a review of surrogacy by the Supreme Court or uniform legislation is generated, law, medicine, ethics, and clinical practice will be in tension and harm may occur, not necessarily because of the practice of surrogacy, but because of the conflicted context in which surrogacy is practiced.

·6·

Conclusions

Although the Supreme Court of New Jersey, in its review of the Baby M case, clearly rejected the commercialization of surrogacy and affirmed the rights of the biological mother, other social and ethical issues remain unresolved. At issue also is whether and to what extent other jurisdictions follow the lead of the New Jersey Supreme Court. But regardless of what one thinks of the decision, we have been given another way of viewing surrogacy.

In this chapter, which stands in agreement with the New Jersey Supreme Court, I will review and summarize the arguments against the practice of surrogate motherhood developed in the book. While no single argument in itself may be a definitive case against the practice of surrogacy, their cumulative weight does make this case.

HUMAN BODY USE

If anything is clear about surrogacy, it is that the practice involves the use of human bodies. Surrogacy can be located within the tradition of the use of bodies such as wet nursing, organ transplantation, blood donation, and participation in research. The practice also is located at the intersection of public and private behavior. These issues provide one level for the analysis of surrogacy.

First, using the distinction between private and public behavior to blunt a critique of surrogacy does not work. By its nature surrogacy touches on issues that are critical for the individual

149

and society and its well-being. How individuals obtain blood or organs is not simply a question of individuals satisfying private needs. It is also a question of how and on what basis individuals are cared for and how society allocates resources. While there are no policies mandating that specific individuals participate in research, progress in medicine requires the participation of human subjects and social well-being is dependent on such participation.

Yet if structures that encourage such participation are coercive or manipulative, subjects will be harmed and may not continue to participate in research. Individuals may not give the gift of their organs if policies and practices allow other people to profit financially from their gift. The differences between the British and American systems for obtaining blood show, in Titmuss's judgment, striking differences when acts of generosity are commercialized or are put in a commercialized context. And the Continental history of wet nursing showed problematic consequences because of its commercialization. Thus acts of individuals have significant and long-lasting social consequences that the distinction between private and public seeks to conceal.

Additionally, these historical analogies suggest that once one commercializes the human body, its parts or its use, problems enter in. First, one begins a process of reducing the body to an object. While it is certainly true that the body is objective and is correctly perceived as an object in some circumstances—a medical examination or operation—to experience it primarily as an object is to diminish its significance and, ultimately, the status of the person who is present to the world through the body. Even when dead, or present as an organ to be transplanted, the body is not simply an object, but, because of its transcendent relation to the person, is a sign of the person's presence in the world.[1] The human body and its separate parts maintain their own dignity, even when separate from the person.

Second, when, as Marx Wartofsky says, one begins "doing it for the money,"[2] a new relation is set up with the person and his or her body: alienation. Karl Marx and Wartofsky both see prostitution as the prototype of alienation. In this act one takes what is most intimate to one's self and then objectifies, prices, and sells it. This objectifies one's body and distances one's self from it, thereby destroying the psychosomatic unity. Ultimately this destroys one's self.

Third, the objectifying and pricing of the body leads to a loss of its dignity. In a fulfillment of the Cartesian vision, the body becomes an extended object, a machine whose parts are interchangeable with any other parts. The body is simply another object in the world alongside other objects; when one part wears out, we simply buy another. Clearly, we know from experience, as Thomas Murray noted, that body parts have a price.[3] Blood and sperm can legally be sold. Other parts are in fact bought and sold on a somewhat open market. To be sure, this is illegal at present, but it is done. But our society has drawn the line by being unwilling to establish a policy of selling bodies and their parts.

Should society allow the body to become commodified and seek its market value, the body would become an object and have a price rather than a dignity. This would substantively contribute to the loss of human dignity. Such a policy would enhance the already common experience of alienation by stating in a policy what many already believe to be true: that their personal worth is only equal to their market value. This experience and policies that reinforce it will only be destructive of human dignity and human solidarity in both the short and long run. Permitting surrogates to be paid contributes to the tendency to price the body and to alienate women from themselves and their bodies.

Additionally, given already prevalent social values, women are frequently seen as objects. Witness their reduction to their physical attributes, their complexion, their hair color, and their alleged ability to enhance the desirability of a product. The practice of surrogacy reinforces this objectification of the woman.

First, the physical appearance of the surrogate is important. Surrogates are selected from a photo album or from a personal interview. How she presents herself is critical. Second, a demonstrated capacity successfully to reproduce is required. Her value comes from a biological capacity. Third, in renting or selling her uterus, the woman is reducing herself to the status of an incubator. Obviously pregnancy is an objective biological process. But it is not only that, for an organic relation develops between fetus and woman that cannot be discounted or ignored. The fetus is not in the woman's body as are her kidneys or lungs or any other organ of her own body. Thus to make of herself only an incubator is to discount the biological processes that are occurring and their impact on her, even after the pregnancy is ended. Fourth, in so renting her uterus the surrogate is assuming the role of a reproductive prostitute.[4] The social and biological analogies between prostitution and surrogacy, even though somewhat harsh, are too obvious to ignore. The surrogate is valued for a biological service she can perform; she is not desired for her person; she is to exit when the job is done; and she is paid. Thus, like the prostitute, the surrogate takes a capacity intimate to herself, objectifies it, prices it, and puts it on the market. This alienates her from herself, makes her a commodity among other commodities, and destroys her dignity.

The practice of surrogacy will destroy women by making objects of them, giving them a price but not a dignity, reinforcing the already present valuing of women primarily for their physical characteristics, and defining their value primarily as an exchange value.

THE COERCION OF THE
NURTURING PARENTS AND THE SURROGATE

Coercion is a difficult concept and one not uniformly applicable to each situation. This is especially true when considering cash or other economic incentives to engage in various activities, for money has a diminishing marginal utility. Some individuals who are extremely wealthy can never have enough and some extremely poor people are content with very little. In thinking about coercion and surrogacy, one has to examine thematic issues as well as the individual situation.

First, to what extent is childbearing itself coercive? Judith Blake's argument that our society has a pronatalist bias needs to be seriously considered.[5] For if it is the case that our status as adults and mature membership in human society depend on having a child, our society may indeed have a pronatalist bias. This bias will exert subtle and unsubtle pressures on women, particularly since they are socially marginalized to begin with. For a woman, then, childbearing can provide a double function.

First, it gives her social value because she has fulfilled her function and, second, it confers upon her adult status. The more that these motivations—even though unconscious—drive a woman, the less free and more coerced her choice with respect to childbearing becomes regardless of whether she is a surrogate or not.

Second, acts become coercive when they contain the threat of harm. There are two sets of harms associated with childbearing, somewhat at odds with each other in the surrogacy context. Childbearing contains some risk of harms that may argue against bearing a child. A certain degree of morbidity is typically, though not always, associated with pregnancy and delivery. There is also a small, but real, risk of mortality. Even if one argues that there is a large dose of cultural conditioning in a woman's choice to have a child, that does not mitigate the harms that are part of that process. The other harm—social as opposed to physical—is the harm of childlessness. In addition to diminished social status, the woman may experience severe strains because of perceptions of a lack of self-worth, of personal failure, and the perception of rejection associated with childlessness. Thus the nurturing mother may be driven to a surrogate by a need to avoid the physical harms of the pregnancy for whatever reasons or to avoid the social harm of childlessness. Also the surrogate may be driven by the desire to have children so she can feel fulfilled and socially useful. Both may be coerced into acts and relations that otherwise they may not have chosen.

Third, the research of Philip Parker, M.D., shows that the primary motivation for surrogates is economic compensation.[6] While the lump-sum payment seems large—ten thousand dollars is the usually quoted fee—it averages out to about $1.50 an hour. We are not talking about an eight-hour shift, five days a week; one is pregnant twenty-four hours a day for about nine months. The fee is well below minimum wage and assumedly such a small amount could not be coercive.

Or could it? First, the worth of the money is determined by one's situation. For some, this may be their way out of a desperate situation, but for others it may simply be extra cash to augment an already comfortable situation. Second, the money is typically provided in one or two payments. A payment of five or ten thousand dollars may be more than an individual has ever received or seen at one time. Third, I suspect few people actually calculate the payment on a per-hour-of-pregnancy basis. Thus ten thousand dollars is perceived much differently than $1.50 an hour.

Finally, the purpose of the prohibition of pre- or immediately postbirth contracts for adoption is precisely designed to avoid any appearance of coercion at a time when the individual is vulnerable emotionally or physically. The prohibitions exist to give some psychological and moral space around the decision of whether or not to give a child up for adoption. Such contracts serve to diminish any coercive elements in this decision. One can argue that since the surrogate contract is made before pregnancy, it is at a sufficient distance from relinquishment of the child so that coercion is not a factor. However, the circumstances of the woman's life—economic, need for social affirmation, or fear of childlessness, for example—may be such that the offer is one she can refuse only with the greatest difficulty because her situation may have coercive elements in it. Additionally, the experience of pregnancy and birth may change the perspective of the woman completely and she may want to keep the child.

While the intent should always be to keep a contract, the situation of surrogacy may qualify such an intent. Many adoption agreements, for example, allow for a change of mind within a certain period of time. Such provisions, while surely difficult on the adopting couple, recognize the difficulty and complexity of the situation and attempt to make provision for it. Even though the surrogate, for example, typically agrees not to bond with the child, such a promise may be impossible to keep even biologically. The surrogate may find herself in a situation in which, if she keeps the contract, she may cause herself significant emotional damage but, if she does not, she will cause serious emotional damage to the genetic father and nurturing mother. Such a conflict may be so disruptive as to make the surrogate unable to make any choices or act in what others might consider a responsible fashion. Either choice produces harm and neither resolves the harms. Whatever choice is made by the woman or is made for her by the court might, in fact, be a coerced decision: a decision in which there are no alternatives, in which harm comes from the choice, and in which control for the choice is out of the surrogate's hands.

The coercive nature of childbearing is uncertain. Part of the uncertainty comes from not knowing the degree to which the culture overrides the choices of individuals and/or blunts their freedom. Also money has a diminishing marginal utility. As well, there is simply a paucity of data to help resolve the issue. Finally, the surrogate may find herself in a situation in which she had no choices whatsoever and all decision-making power is taken from her.

The coupling of an apparently large fee for being a surrogate with the identified primary economic motivation of surrogates creates a situation that is potentially coercive. The loss of such a fee by not being a surrogate may be experienced as an actual harm and thus be coercive. Otherwise the fee may serve as either an inducement or a bribe, neither of which are, of course, associated with high moral standards. Thus at best the fee responds to an articulated motivation of potential surrogates. As such it creates a context in which the potential surrogate may act against her own best interests and in fact may be coerced or unfairly induced. By being paid, the surrogate enters into a compromised context and becomes vulnerable if she is not aware of her own interests, needs, and motivations. Not paying a fee would eliminate many but not all of the moral concerns. Additionally, the harms that may come to the surrogate from either fulfilling the contract or from not fulfilling it may in fact so diminish her decision-making capacities that her choices are simply not free choices. The whole surrogacy process occurs within a context that has coercive elements attached to it. One must examine each case separately to accurately ascertain whether there are coercive elements in it and to what extent they are operative.

BABY SELLING

In the practice of surrogacy, a couple contracts for a woman to become pregnant and then relinquish the baby to them postbirth when the terms of the contract have been fulfilled, that is, when the couple receive the child they want. For this the woman is given a cash payment. If the terms of the contract are not fulfilled, the cash is not given, or, for example, in the event of a miscarriage a partial payment is made. The exchange of cash is dependent upon the couple's obtaining the child they want.

The prosurrogacy camp argues that this is nothing but reimbursement for services provided. There is a partial truth here in that the biological father typically pays for the health care services utilized by the genetic-nurturing mother. The untested issue—fortunately—is whether the biological father could sue for recovery of these costs in the event the contract were not fulfilled in some way.

The biological father does not pay the surrogate fee when the contract is not fulfilled either because of claims that the child was not his or because the surrogate refused to relinquish the child. Assumedly, most people would think this is reasonable since the contract was not fulfilled.

The fulfillment of the surrogate contract essentially consists in the production by the genetic-nurturing mother of an acceptable child who is then taken by the biological father. When this occurs, a fee is exchanged. This is exchanging cash for a baby. In a debate on surrogacy, Angela Holder captured this point well when she argued that when you go into a store, ask for an item, and pay for it when the clerk hands it to you, you have bought it and it is yours. You have not purchased the services of the clerk, though to be sure some of the payment is the basis of his or her salary. You have purchased the item and you have it and a receipt saying you paid for it. If someone would try to take it away from you, this would be an act of theft for which that individual could be arrested and prosecuted. In surrogacy, cash changes hands and the baby changes families.[7]

If there is some relevant difference between fulfilling the terms of a contract by receiving some item when cash is exchanged upon receiving it and fulfilling the terms of a surrogacy contract by exchanging cash when the baby is relinquished, I truly fail to see it. In either case, money is exchanged for an object which then passes to a new owner when the terms of the contract are fulfilled. I even think Noel Keane admits as much when he suggests that, even if surrogacy were a commercial exchange, fulfilling needs and wants in this way simply happens to be the way we do things in a commercialized society.[8] And surely he is correct. In our commercialized society we do indeed fulfill our needs and wants through commercial relations.

But from the fact that we buy and sell many—perhaps even

most—things, it neither follows that we should sell everything nor that we are correct in selling what we already sell. If we accept the commercial model uncritically, we may fall into the danger of knowing the price of everything and the value of nothing. Additionally, by pricing babies in this fashion, we are making an explicit frontal assault on human dignity and the moral worth of an individual. Such pricing of an individual, by its nature reduces the individual to what he or she can be exchanged for on the market. The only worth, in this perspective, is economic worth. Any transcendental dimension of the person is diminished, if not disregarded, by such a pricing mechanism.

The surrogate contract is, in essence, a contract to buy or sell a child and should be prohibited. Such practices, as Angela Holder observes, are prohibited by the Thirteenth Amendment which outlaws the selling of humans.[9] Such a constitutional provision would, in my judgment, outweigh claims of rights to privacy and the right to reproduce derivitive from the right to privacy. In addition to the Thirteenth Amendment's prohibition on selling persons, the state also has the right to restrict even constitutional rights when there is a compelling state interest to do so. Surely trafficking in babies would present such a compelling state interest.

FEMINIST PERSPECTIVES

Of special concern are the implications of surrogacy for women. In particular is the question of what surrogacy says about the role of women. Surrogacy reinforces the still prevalent cultural stereotype that values women primarily, if not exclusively, for their reproductive function. This reduces the value of a woman to her physiology and specifically her reproductive capacity. Her person is lost and she has no dignity except that which accrues from the impersonality of biology.

The practice of surrogacy further denigrates the infertile woman. In essence, she is told that since she simply cannot meet her partner's need to have a child genetically related to him, he has to go out and rent a woman who can do this for him. Again, the primary value of the woman is reproductive capacity. Although many report that wives freely cooperate with this process, one has to wonder whether or not this is a survival mechanism. And even if the woman participates in the surrogacy situation to save the marriage or to keep her husband, what is this saying about the status of the woman, the dominance of the male, and the nature of this marriage?

Second, by agreeing to be a surrogate, a woman buys into the most narrow understanding of freedom: the freedom to buy and sell. While no one should dictate what women can and cannot do, we should attend to the understanding of freedom that women may literally be buying into in becoming surrogates. The freedom that money and access to it brings contributes enormously to our sense of well-being. Freedom from financial burdens and freedom to obtain one's needs and wants remove stress and allow one to have many of the advantages our culture provides. Yet if the freedom to buy or sell is the only or primary freedom, our lives would be poverty stricken. We would compromise, for example, our freedoms with respect to career choice, to participate in cultural activities, to relocate, to begin a new job, to be responsible for our actions.

Many of these freedoms require, obviously, an economic underpinning. But if the major or most desirable understanding of freedom is the ability to buy and sell, the majority of significant life experiences have been lost. To reduce freedom to only one aspect, and to such a narrow one at that, is to destroy freedom. Thus one must carefully examine the dangers of the siren song of freedom promised by the surrogacy contract. One might also ask whether men would be content with their ability to sell a biological capacity as the apex of their freedom. And the answer to that question might just be the most profound commentary on surrogacy.

Finally, and in a related context, surrogacy bears a close relation to prostitution. In prostitution the woman sells or rents a body part; the relation is impersonal; the woman does the man's bidding; her value is a function she performs; and she is to leave when the job is done. The surrogate mother does the same things. The only difference is that with the surrogate intercourse is typically technical, whereas with the prostitute both biological and technical means are used. And of course the surrogate is expected to become pregnant and the prostitute is not.

The context in which surrogacy is practiced seems to blunt the comparison with prostitution. After all, surrogacy is arranged in an attorney's office; the surrogate has been cleared with reference to her intelligence, appearance, and physical and psychological health; the motives are to help a couple to have what most other married couples have. Yet when this veneer is stripped away, the analogy with prostitution is right there. For the surrogate is selected essentially on the basis of desirable criteria, is paid to provide her body, and is then dumped. Many then complete the analogy by identifying the broker as the pimp. Many of the attorneys involved in this work understandably are unhappy with this label. But if the analogy between surrogacy and prostitution holds, then those associated with its practice must be expected to assume their proper position also.

Finally, surrogacy can contribute to the social stereotyping of women. Frequently in our culture, women are valued primarily because of their reproductive capacity and have social status through fulfilling social roles assumedly derived from that capacity. While it is true that women gestate the fetus, it does not follow that their full human worth is defined from that biological fact nor that such a biological capacity either confers specific characteristics or defines social roles. Plainly stated, the fact that something occurs in nature as a biological reality does not mean that that event is normative for human behavior. In fact, frequently we humans pride ourselves on acting against what occurs in nature: the killing of the young, forced and impersonal matings, the rule of the physically strong, and the giving of primacy to the group rather than the individual.

The responsibility for nurturing the young is an extremely important one. But the primary or main responsibility for this does not accrue to the woman because she has physically given birth. Surrogacy is in a paradoxical situation here. For it clearly affirms the split between reproduction and nurturing, but values the genetic-carrying mother only for that biological capacity, and it might suggest that the nurturing and socialization will be done primarily by the nurturing mother, the biological father having done his share by providing the sperm. Thus surrogacy functions to keep women in their place, a place frequently not chosen by them and, even if chosen, a place often devalued or rejected by the more market-driven values of our society. The ultimate irony is that while the practice of surrogacy may provide some women with the opportunity to achieve their desires and wants, it does this only through reducing other women to their biological functions and by reenforcing cultural stereotypes about women.

FAMILIAL ISSUES

If there is one institution that has demonstrated a capacity to appear and function in a variety of forms, it is the family. Defining the family without reference to a particular historical and/or cultural context is notoriously difficult. The family we know today is not the family that was nor is it the family that will be. The family is dramatically changing right before our eyes in the light of various liberation movements. The practice of surrogacy obviously raises issues of importance to the family.

Surrogacy establishes an intentional separation of the roles connected with marriage and parenthood. That these roles are separable is not news and that they can be fulfilled in a variety of ways is not particularly noteworthy. The socially accepted practice of adoption and the overlapping of several roles in the extended family provide models of successful ways of nurturing and rearing a child. What is unique about surrogacy is that typically the woman who provides the egg and carries the pregnancy has no prebirth relation with the biological father and according to contract will have nothing to do with the child postbirth.

Such a practice raises issues with respect to the child's lineage. We know that some children who have been adopted and some who have been born of artificial insemination by donor wish to know who their biological parent was. While this is not true of all such children, it is true of a large number of them. Is it fair to the child to introduce such a potentially problematic situation into his or her life? Lineage is an important issue and perhaps runs deeper in us than we assume. The practice of surrogacy needs careful consideration with respect to that significant element in our lives before we wholeheartedly accept it.

Second, there have been a small number of reported cases in which the surrogate was also the sister of the nurturing mother. Such a situation raises two sets of problems. On the one hand, what is society to make of the biologically fused roles of mother-aunt? This is different than the diffusing of roles in the extended family in that even though the roles may overlap in practice, the people who occupy them are biologically distinct and everyone knows who is who and the limitation on behavior based on the precise knowledge of such roles. When the roles are biologically fused, this may not be so easy to do. On the other hand, will the surrogate mother-sister be able fully to relinquish the child to her sister? This will be particularly important with respect to child-rearing practices in the event that there is a difference of philosophy between them. While in practice the surrogate mother-sister may have physically delivered the child to her sister, psychological deliverance may not be so simple.

Third, given the fact that surrogates are preferred to have had prior children to demonstrate the quality of their reproductive capacities, what effects might the relinquishment of the child by the surrogate have on her own children? There are no data that I am aware of to help answer this question. The answer may in part depend on the age and development of the children. It may depend on how the surrogate explains it to them. But we must take its possible impact on the children of the surrogate into account. Children already have a variety of fears and anxieties about the loss of parents. They have fears of their being lost, abandoned, or being kidnaped. Seeing their mother go through a pregnancy and then sell the baby could raise fears about the stability of their own situation. This is an exceptionally urgent question which needs careful consideration and evaluation before we get any deeper into the surrogacy business.

A final issue, and one which can be addressed fully only from the perspective of a longitudinal review of experience, is the effect of surrogacy on the surrogate's husband and the genetic father's wife. These are the two people who are out of the research loop in studies of the reproductive technologies. With respect to the surrogate's husband, several issues are important to consider. First, how does he feel about his wife's carrying another person's child? Although this question smacks of his asserting property rights over his wife, her uterus, and its contents, the question has an authentic moral and psychological value. Typically, and for reasons that transcend property issues, when a husband finds his wife pregnant by someone else, that is a clear sign of an adulterous relation and the alienation of affection. As such this could be more than ample grounds for a divorce. The surrogacy relation is different in that the pregnancy is established technically and with consent, and there is *prima facie* no relation other than contractual with the genetic father. Nonetheless the carrying of the child of another is not simply a neutral experience. It is a critical somatic reality that will last nine months. What will this experience mean to the surrogate's husband? Second, pregnancy typically is a psychosomatic reality which affects the relation between husband and wife who are also becoming father and mother. The pregnancy causes the couple to rework and reestablish many elements of their previous relationship as the basis on which they establish their new role as parents. Thus the desire for the pregnancy, its meaningfulness for the couple, and its reconstituting them as a new social unit give them the capacity to deal with the demands of the pregnancy. Within the surrogacy situation, only the biological elements of this dynamic will be present and essentially only for the surrogate. What motivation does her husband have to go through this process with her? For clearly the pregnancy will place demands on their marriage, yet stands outside of any developmental process that typically gives meaning to the routine physical discomforts and implications of pregnancy.

Second, what has brought the spouse or partner of the genetic father to cooperate with this situation? Is it fear of a divorce; is it a desire to please the husband; is it out of concern for a traditional family; is it out of desire for a child? Obviously these issues cannot be as neatly separated as I have just suggested. But on the other hand, they raise issues that have not been attended to. An analogous situation might be the development of penile implants. While such implants brought benefits to impotent males, their significance for and impact on women has not been studied. Since their benefits were so obvious for men, why include any others in an examination of their effects? Women have historically engaged in a variety of activities to please, placate, or soothe males, especially when the egos of males were perceived to be threatened. The practice of surrogacy may be another continuation of this practice. A critical area for study is to determine who initiates the proposed use of surrogates. Such a finding may reveal much about the socialization of women and their status within marriage.

Having a child is not only a biological experience. Having someone else's child within the context of a marriage, is neither morally neutral nor merely biological. Having a child is to say something about one's self, one's relations with others, and to take on certain responsibilities. To reject all of these dimensions, to deny the moral implications of surrogacy on one's marriage, and to neglect the implications of our bodily dimensions for our psychic well-being is to cut off a rather large part of our reality. Surrogacy assumes this can be done with no remainder. The continuing aftermath of the effects of the Baby M case on Mary Beth Whitehead, particularly her divorce and remarriage, may be testimony to this.

THE RIGHT TO HAVE CHILDREN

Another contested issue is the claim of a right to have children.[10] To understand this argument, we need to distinguish between legal and moral rights and positive and negative rights. Simply stated, legal rights are those rights which are given to the individual because some specific law states he or she has them. Moral rights are those which accrue to the person because of a moral argument based on the nature of the person and are present irrespective of any law. Positive rights confer a duty on another to ensure that I can fulfill my right. A negative right requires that I not be interfered with as I seek my rights and thus establishes claims of noninterference. Determining whether or not one has legal rights and their extent is relatively easy; the determination of moral rights is not as easy.

There is both a legal and moral right to reproduce. Historically, philosophically, and theologically, children have been seen as a good in themselves and as the fruit of marriage. To prohibit the seeking of such a good is a violation of the person and such a moral right to reproduce is protected in a variety of ways in our legal system.

Is the right to procreate a positive or negative right? Legally and morally, the right to reproduce is a negative one. That is,

the right is typically secured by the fact that *prima facie* no one
may interfere with or prohibit one from seeking the exercise of
that right. That is, given the fact that children are a good and
that the individual has certain privacy rights, some restrictions
on their actions are inappropriate. There is a liberty of action,
a zone of privacy, and the inherent dignity of the person that
must be respected. This is done by securing his or her liberty of
action.

The right to reproduce does not include the right actually to
obtain a child. What is protected legally and morally is the right
to exercise a capacity, not the securing of the end of that capacity.
It is not the obligation of law, philosophy, medicine, or theology
to guarantee that one actually achieve that for which one strives.
What is minimally required is that one not be interfered with in
attempting to attain a goal. The right to free speech does not
require that one be listened to, simply that one be able to speak.
The right to life requires that one be secure in his or her person.
It does not guarantee a security system in one's home. One's civil
rights entitle one to decent social treatment, not to a guaranteed
reservation at the best restaurant in the country. The right to
medical treatment requires appropriate care, not the services of
every specialist within a fifty-mile radius.

Similarly, the right to reproduce does not ensure those exercising that right that they will receive a child. Infertility, to borrow
a phrase from H. Tristram Engelhardt, is unfortunate, but not
unfair.[11] For individuals wishing a child, infertility is frequently
a crushing blow. Yet no sense of justice has been violated because
of this biological incapacity. Such an incapacity may be inconvenient, depressing, frustrating, and even destructive of a relationship, but the fact that a couple is infertile does not constitute
a violation of justice. There is simply no argument which guarantees an individual even an average biological constitution in
the natural lottery through which we are given our body.

Thus while there is a legally and morally protected right to
procreate, there is no similar right which guarantees the obtaining
of a child through the exercise of such a right. While unfortunate
and tragic for the individuals involved, they have not been morally wronged by the fact of their infertility. But should society
or the private sector help individuals secure the good they desire?

First, the fact that any biological deficiencies from the natural lottery do not constitute a violation of justice diminishes any claim to positive assistance. Second, the fact that the possession of a right guarantees its exercise, not its accomplishment, also suggests that justice is not necessarily violated by a failure to gain the goal of the right. Third, even though there is a right to reproduce, there is debate over whether having a child is a need or a want. And if having a child is determined to be a need, we must still consider whether this need is social or individual. If, therefore, the need is social—to guarantee the continuation of society—it may be fulfilled by the fact that some couples have children. Thus individual claims to social or private assistance would be weakened. Finally, we typically expect that the health care system will respond to us and our needs. And by and large the system has done this even though health resources are not distributed in a totally equitable fashion. We assume that when ill we will be taken care of to the limit of the technology available. I fear we have erroneously inferred that since we are typically cared for in this way, we are indeed entitled to such treatment, that we indeed have a positive right to such treatment. Such an argument logically doesn't work. And as the cost of health care continues to spiral out of control, we will find that arguments based on custom will not carry very much moral or legal weight.

However, this does not mean that society or the private sector need do nothing. Society, through the legislative process, may determine that individual procreative choices rank higher than other social goods—for example, the development of the artificial heart, the space program, or federally sponsored sex education programs. Society may then choose to assist such individuals in obtaining a child through utilizing any of the birth technologies. Such a decision would be based on social desires, not claims in justice. Additionally, the private sector in the form of an insurance company or an individual physician may make arrangements with their clients to provide these services. An insurance company may choose to pay for IVF, but it will also charge a premium for it. An individual physician may provide IVF but it will be on a traditional fee for service basis. Again, what we have here is the exercise of liberty rights, not securing a service based on claims of justice or welfare rights.

There is indeed a legally and morally established and protected right to reproduce or procreate, but that is as far as the right goes. Individuals may not claim that their right to reproduce has been violated if they obtain no child or if society or the private sector does not come to their assistance by providing either money or programs to help them utilize various birth technologies. The fact of infertility is unfortunate, but individuals have not suffered an injustice if they are infertile.

SUMMARY

In my judgment, these arguments constitute a strong case against the practice of surrogate motherhood. The practice is inherently problematic from a practical and moral perspective. Its utilization continues the social disenfranchisement of women, puts the child at the risk of existing in a compromised social and familial context, and simply encourages the commodification of women and children. I can only conclude that the practice of surrogate motherhood should be prohibited.

Notes

Chapter 1. The Technologies of Surrogate Mothering

1. J. B. S. Haldane, *Daedalus or Science and the Future* (New York: E. P. Dutton and Co., 1924), pp. 63–65.
2. Ibid., pp. 66–67.
3. Aldous Huxley, *Brave New World* (New York: Harper & Row, Perennial Library, 1946), p. 4.
4. Gen. 16:1–4.
5. Gen. 16:5–6.
6. Gen. 29:31.
7. Gen. 30:1–24.
8. P. C. Steptoe and R. G. Edwards, "Birth After the Reimplantation of a Human Embryo," *Lancet*, 12 August 1978, p. 366.
9. G. Pincus and E. V. Enzman, "Can Mammalian Eggs Undergo Normal Development in Vitro?," *Academy Science* 20 (1934):21.
10. M. C. Chang, "Normal Development of Fertilized Rabbit Ova Stored at Low Temperature for Several Days," *Nature* 161 (1948):978.
11. A general overview of this process can be found in Clifford Grobstein, "External Human Fertilization," *Scientific American* 240 (June 1979):57–67. More technical articles are: M. I. Evans, A. B. Mukherjee, and J. D. Schuman, "Human In Vitro Fertilization," *Obstetrical and Gynecological Survey* 35 (1980):71–81; and A. Lopata, I. Johnson, I. Hoult, and A. Spiers, "Pregnancy Following Intrauterine Implanation of an Embryo Obtained by In Vitro Fertilization of a Preovulated Egg," *Fertility and Sterility* 33 (February 1980):117–20.
12. Evans et al., "Human In Vitro Fertilization," pp. 76–77.
13. It is difficult, in our rapidly changing times, to know what to call sexual intercourse, without indicating some philosophical position. Thus the term "natural intercourse" may indicate that this form is also normative and that alternative modes of achieving conception are un-

167

natural and, therefore, wrong. As an attempt to resolve this problem, I shall use the term "customary intercourse" to refer to sexual intercourse as it is usually understood and practiced by two heterosexuals.

14. C. Grobstein, M. Flower, and J. Mendeloff, "External Human Fertilization: An Evaluation of Policy," *Science* 222 (14 October 1983):127–33.

15. M. Bustillo, J. E. Buster, S. E. Cohen, et al., "Non-surgical Ovum Transfer as a Treatment in Infertile Women: Preliminary Experience," *Journal of the American Medical Association* 251 (1984):1171–73.

16. Peter Singer and Deane Wells, *Making Babies: The New Science and Ethics of Conception* (New York: Charles Scribner's Sons, 1985), p. 83.

17. Lori Andrews, *New Conceptions: A Consumers Guide to the Newest Infertility Treatments* (New York: Ballantine Books, 1985), p. 238.

18. Ibid.

19. Ibid., pp. 222ff.

Chapter 2. Moral Analogues to Surrogate Mothering

1. Richard M. Titmuss, *The Gift Relation: From Human Blood to Human Policy* (New York: Pantheon Books, 1971).

2. Ibid., 78–88.

3. Ibid., 94.

4. Ibid., 94.

5. Ibid., 89.

6. These are based on Titmuss's summary of recommendations made in *The Price of Blood* by M. H. Cooper and A. J. Culyer (London: the Institute of Economic Affairs, 1968), and in Titmuss, *The Gift Relation,* p. 195. These authors conclude their study with the following conclusions: (1) Blood is an economic good and subject to economic analysis. (2) Pricing of blood is feasible. (3) One can attach precise economic meaning to wastage. (4) Payment to donors in a dual system would increase supply by encouraging more donors to come forward and would provide an incentive to paid donors to donate more frequently. (5) There is a lack of knowledge about the motivations of donors and nondonors. (6) Of the choice between paying for blood or removing obstacles to donating, it is unclear which is less costly. (7) In debate for and against payment, economic analysis cannot establish implications not written into the assumptions of the analysis. Nonetheless, one can diagnose waste and shortage and conclude that economic action through pricing would help eliminate them.

7. Ibid., p. 180.

8. Ibid.
9. Ibid., p. 240.
10. Ibid., p. 158.
11. Ibid., p. 198.
12. Ibid., p. 171.
13. Ibid., p. 170.
14. Ibid., pp. 217–18.
15. For an overview of some of the ethical issues raised by the use of humans in research, confer Jay Katz, *Experimentation with Human Beings* (New York: Russell Sage Foundation, 1972), and Bernard Barber, *Research on Human Subjects: Problems of Social Control in Medical Experimentation* (New York: Russell Sage Foundation, 1973). Also the journal *IRB: A Review of Human Subjects Research*, available through the Hastings Center, provides articles on current issues of the ethics of the use of humans in research.
16. Titmuss, *The Gift Relation*, pp. 225–26.
17. Ibid., pp. 245–46.
18. Arthur Caplan, "Ethical Issues in the Procurement of Cadaver Organs for Transplantation," *New England Journal of Medicine* 311 (11 October 1984):982.
19. Luke Skelley, "Practical Issues in Obtaining Organs for Transplantation," *Law, Medicine, and Health Care* 13 (February 1985):36.
20. Stuart J. Younger et. al., "Psychosocial and Ethical Implications of Organ Retrieval," *New England Journal of Medicine* 313 (August 1985):322.
21. Marvin Brahms, "Transplantable Human Organs: Should Their Sale Be Authorized by State Statutes?," *Americal Journal of Law and Medicine* 3 (Summer 1977):186.
22. Ibid., p. 190. Emphasis in original.
23. Ibid.
24. Ibid., pp. 191–92.
25. Ibid., pp. 192–93.
26. "The Sale of Human Body Parts," *Michigan Law Review* 72 (May 1974):1182–1264 and 1222–23.
27. Ibid., pp. 1225–26.
28. George Annas, "Life, Liberty, and the Pursuit of Organ Sales," *Hastings Center Report* 14 (February 1984):23.
29. Roberta G. Simmons, Susan D. Klein, and Richard L. Simmons, *Gift of Life: The Social and Psychological Impact of Organ Transplantation* (New York: John Wiley and Sons, 1977), p. 35.
30. Frances H. Miller, "Reflections on Organ Transplantation in the U.K.," *Law, Medicine, and Health Care* 13 (February 1985):32.

31. Annas, "Life, Liberty, and the Pursuit of Organ Sales," p. 23.

32. William F. May, "Attitudes Toward the Newly Dead," Hastings Center *Studies* 1 (1973):8. For an updated version of this article, see "Religion and the Donation of Body Parts," Hastings Center *Report* 15 (February 1985):38–42.

33. Paul Ramsey, *The Patient as Person* (New Haven: Yale University Press, 1970), p. 210.

34. William F. May, "Attitudes," p. 12.

35. "The Sale of Human Body Parts," pp. 1228–30. This paragraph summarizes the arguments of this section of the article.

36. Here I am following the line of reasoning developed by Ruth Macklin in "On Paying Money to Research Subjects," *IRB: A Review of Human Subjects Research* 3 (May 1981):1–6. Professor Macklin, in general, argues that cash payments can be limited. A critical response to this is Lisa Newton's "Inducement, Due and Otherwise," *IRB: A Review of Human Subjects Research* 4 (March 1982):4–6.

37. Macklin, "On Paying Money," p. 2

38. Marx Wartofsky, "On Doing It for Money," in *Research Involving Prisoners*, Appendix to Report and Recommendations, the National Commission for the Protection of Human Subjects of Biomedical and Behavioral Research, 1976, DHEW Publication no. (OS) 76–132, p. 3–3. This article is also available in Thomas A. Mappes and Jane S. Zembaty, *Biomedical Ethics* (New York: McGraw-Hill, 1981), pp. 186–94. This article is not available in the second edition.

39. Ibid., pp. 3–13.

40. Ibid., pp. 3–18.

41. Ibid., pp. 3–19.

42. Ibid., pp. 3–21.

43. Ibid., pp. 3–21.

44. Ibid., pp. 3–19.

45. George D. Sussman, *Selling Mothers' Milk: The Wet Nursing Business in France, 1715–1914* (Urbana, IL: University of Illinois Press, 1982), p. 2. Confer also Ian Wickes, "A History of Infant Feeding," *Archives of Diseases in Childhood* 28 (1953):151–58; 232–40; 416–22; 495–502.

46. Sussman, *Selling Mothers' Milk,* p. 2. A series of articles, primarily on the history of childhood, which discusses aspects of wet nursing can be found in Lloyd DeMause, ed., *The History of Childhood* (New York: Psychohistory Press, 1974).

47. Lloyd DeMause, "The Evolution of Childhood," in *The History of Childhood, p. 34.*

48. Ibid., p. 9.

49. Ibid., p. 10.

50. Joseph E. Illick, "Child Rearing in Seventeenth-Century England and America," in *The History of Childhood*, pp. 309ff.

51. Francesco da Barberino (1264–1348), *Reggimento e costumi di donna*, quoted from James Bruce Ross, "The Middle Class Child in Urban Italy, Fourteenth to Early Sixteenth Century," in *The History of Childhood*, p. 190.

52. Edward Shorter, *The Making of the Modern Family* (New York: Basic Books, 1975), 178–79.

53. Confer the articles by McLaughlin, Ross, Marvick, Illick, and Dunn in *The History of Childhood* and the demographic studies compiled by Sussman, *Selling Mother's Milk*.

54. Cf. Sussman, *Sellings Mothers' Milk*, pp. 136ff., and Shorter, *The Modern Family*, pp. 179ff.

55. Sussman, *Selling Mothers' Milk*, provides a thorough study of this in France where these bureaus frequently worked with the local Catholic parish priest who would certify the qualities of the nurse. Confer Lindemann, *The History of Childhood*, pp. 389ff., for how this was done in Germany.

56. Valerie A. Feldes, *Breasts, Bottles and Babies: A History of Infant Feeding* (Edinburgh: Edinburgh University Press, 1986), pp. 273ff.

57. Ibid., p. 158.

58. Ibid., pp. 152ff.

59. Elizabeth Wirth Marvick, "Nature versus Nurture: Patterns and Trends in Seventeenth Century French Child Rearing," in *The History of Childhood*, p. 265. Confer also Mary Lindemann, "Love for Hire: The Regulation of the Wet-Nursing Business in Eighteenth Century Hamburg," *Journal of Family History* 6 (Winter 1981):379–95, esp. 383–84.

60. James Bruce Ross, in "The Middle Class Child," p. 193, translates one such song, a verse of which goes:

> In every matter, we know what to do,
> so that the baby gows up quickly;
> as long as he stays straight and hard
> we don't mind getting tired;
> and he'll never leave us
> until his nursing is finished:
> so you can be quite confident
> in sending him to the Casentino.

61. Marvick, "Nature Versus Nurture," p. 268.

62. Sergey Aksakov, *Years of Childhood*, trans. Alec Brown (New York: Vintage Books, 1960), p. 3.

63. Illick, "Childbearing in Seventeenth Century England and America," p. 310.

64. Ross, "The Middle Class Child," p. 196.

65. Shorter, *The Modern Family*, p. 185.

66. Shorter cites data suggesting an infant mortality rate ranging between 50 and 67 percent, *The Modern Family*, p. 186. Sussman, *Selling Mothers' Milk*, p. 127, cites studies suggesting a 52 percent infant mortality rate in 1867.

67. Shorter, *The Modern Family*, pp. 185–86.

68. Thomas H. Murray, "Gifts of the Body and the Needs of Strangers," Hastings Center *Report* 17 (April 1987):35.

Chapter 3. Background Moral Issues

1. Edward Shorter, *The Making of the Modern Family* (New York: Basic Books, 1975), p. 29.

2. Ibid.

3. Ibid., p. 227.

4. Ibid., pp. 227–28 and 5.

5. Ibid., p. 7.

6. Gillian Hanscombe, "The Right to Lesbian Parenthood," *Journal of Medical Ethics* 9 (1983):133–35.

7. Jeffery Blumstein, *Parents and Children: The Ethics of the Family* (New York: Oxford University Press, 1982), p. 151.

8. Ibid., pp. 148–49.

9. Ibid., p. 55.

10. The material in this section summarizes data gathered by Edward Pohlman and reported in "Motivations in Wanting Conceptions," in Ellen Peck and Judith Senderowitz, ed., *Pronatalism: The Myth of Mom and Apple Pie* (New York: Thomas Y. Crowell Co., 1974), pp. 159–90.

11. Confer also Harold Feldman, "Changes in Marriage and Parenthood: A Methodological Design," in Peck and Senderowitz, *Pronatalism*, pp. 206–26.

12. Blumstein, *Parents and Children*, p. 150.

13. Martha E. Griminez, "Feminism, Pronatalism, and Motherhood," in Joyce Trebiloc, ed., *Mothering: Essays in Feminist Theory* (Totowa: NJ: Roman and Allanhold, 1983), p. 288. Emphasis in original.

14. Ibid.

15. Peck and Senderowitz, *Pronatalism*, p. 1. Emphasis in the original.

16. Ibid., pp. 3–4.

17. Judith Blake, "Coercive Pronatalism and American Population Policy," in Peck and Senderowitz, *Pronatalism*, p. 30.

18. Blumstein, *Parents and Children*, p. 140.
19. Edgar Page, "Parental Rights," *Journal of Applied Philosophy* 1 (1984):200.
20. Ibid.
21. Ibid., p. 201.
22. Ibid.
23. Ibid., p. 201.
24. Ibid., p. 202. Emphasis in original.
25. Oliver O'Donovan, *Begotten or Made?* (Oxford: Clarendon Press, 1984), p. 2.
26. Ibid., p. 16.
27. Ibid., p. 17.
28. Ibid., p. 77.
29. Gillain Hanscombe, "The Right to Lesbian Parenthood," p. 135.
30. Ibid., p. 133.
31. O'Donovan, *Begotten or Made?*, p. 20.
32. John A. Robertson, "The Right to Procreate and In Utero Therapy," *Journal of Legal Medicine* 3 (1982):335.
33. Ibid., p. 339.
34. Ibid., p. 340.
35. Ibid., pp. 340–41.
36. Ruth Macklin, *Man, Mind, and Morality: The Ethics of Behavioral Control* (Englewood Cliffs, NJ: Prentice-Hall, 1982), p. 12. Confer also her discussion of due and undue inducements in my discussion of human research in chap. 2 of this book.
37. Michael D. Bayles, "A Concept of Coercion," in *Coercion*, ed. J. Roland Pennock and John W. Chapman (Chicago: Aldine-Atherton, Inc., 1972), 16–29.
38. Ibid., p. 18.
39. Ibid., p. 17.
40. Ibid., pp. 28–29.
41. Bernard Gert, "Coercion and Freedom," in *Coercion*, pp. 30–48.
42. Ibid., p. 32.
43. Ibid., p. 31.
44. Ibid., p. 32.
45. Ibid., p. 36.
46. Ibid., p. 44.
47. Ibid., p. 46.
48. Willard Gaylin, "A Psychoanalytic Look at Coercion," *Psychiatry* 37 (February 1974):1–9.
49. Ibid., p. 4. Emphasis in original.

50. Ibid., p. 7.

51. Shulamith Firestone, *The Dialectic of Sex: The Case for Feminist Revolution* (New York: Bantam Books, 1970), p. 229.

52. Ibid.

53. Linda Gordon, *Woman's Body, Woman's Right. A Social History of Birth Control in America* (New York: Grossman Publishers, 1976), pp. 404–5.

54. Judith Blake, "Coercive Pronatalism and American Population Policy," in Peck and Senderowitz, *Pronatalism*, pp. 29–67. In evaluating her argument, one must keep in mind her context: developing a strategy to decrease the American population. Thus in addition to being descriptive, the article is also arguing for specific social changes to achieve a specific social policy. This does not invalidate her argument; it does set it in an important context.

55. Ibid., p. 32.

56. Ibid.

57. Ibid.

58. Ibid., p. 66.

59. Grimez, "Feminism, Pronatalism, and Motherhood," in Trebiloc, ed., *Mothering*, p. 288. In this article Grimez acknowledges her dependence on Blake.

60. Blake, "Coercive Pronatialim and American Population Policy," in Peck and Senderowitz, *Pronatalism*, p. 30.

61. Grimez, "Feminism," in Trebiloc, ed., *Mothering*, p. 290.

62. Ibid. Emphasis in original.

63. This section summarizes her argument on pp. 301–8.

64. Ibid., p. 304.

65. Ibid., p. 306.

66. Andrea Dworkin, *Right-Wing Women* (New York: Coward-McCann, Inc., 1983), p. 15.

67. Ibid., p. 19.

68. This paragraph summarizes material on pp. 21ff. of Dworkin's book.

69. Ibid., p. 104.

70. Blake, "Coercive Pronatalism," in Peck and Senderowitz, *Pronatalism*, p. 32.

71. Gert, "Coercion and Freedom," in *Coercion*, p. 34.

72. Ibid., p. 39.

73. Philip Parker, M.D., "Motivation of Surrogate Mothers: Initial Findings," *American Journal of Psychiatry* 140 (January 1983):117.

74. Ibid., p. 118.

75. Ibid.

76. Ibid.

77. Philip Parker, M.D., "Surrogate Motherhood, Psychiatric Screening and Informed Consent, Baby Selling, and Public Screening," *Bulletin of the American Academy of Psychiatry Law* 12 (1984):21–39. This article includes no new data. Parker refers to the previous article as his data base.

78. Ibid., p. 26.

79. Philip Parker, M.D., "The Psychology of the Pregnant Surrogate Mother: A Newly Updated Report of a Longitudinal Pilot Study," unpublished report presented at the meeting of the American Orthopsychiatric Association, 9 April 1984. Dr. Parker generously provided a copy of this report to me.

80. Ibid., p. 4.

81. Ibid., p. 6.

82. Ibid., p. 9.

83. Ibid., pp. 11–12.

84. Ibid., p. 12.

85. Allen W. Wood, *Karl Marx* (London: Routledge and Kegan Paul, 1981), p. 7.

86. Ibid., p. 8.

87. Ibid., p. 13. Emphasis in original.

88. Ibid.

89. Joachim Israel, *Alienation: From Marx to Modern Sociology* (Atlantic Highlands: NJ: Humanities Press, 1979), p. 41.

90. Ibid.

91. Karl Marx, "Economic and Philosophical Manuscripts," quoted in Israel, *Alienation,* p. 44.

92. Ibid., p. 52.

93. Ibid., p. 58.

94. Ibid., p. 321.

95. Immanuel Kant, *Lectures on Ethics* (Indianapolis, IN: Hackett, 1980), pp. 165–66.

96. C. Wright Mills, *White Collar: The American Middle Classes* (New York: Oxford University Press, 1953).

97. Ibid., pp. 178ff.

98. Ibid., p. 182.

99. Ibid., p. 188.

100. Ten thousand dollars seems to be the fee most quoted and recommended. Nonetheless, one occasionally sees higher fees offered, and since there are no regulations, we have essentially a free market

situation where any price is possible. For example, an ad ran for several months in 1984 in *Boston Magazine* seeking a surrogate at the fee of $50,000.

Chapter 4. Specific Ethical Issues

1. John Robertson, "Surrogate Mothers: Not So Novel After All," Hastings Center *Report* 13 (October 1983):28.
2. R. Snowden, G. D. Mitchell, and E. M. Snowden, *Artificial Reproduction: A Social Investigation* (Longon: George Allen and Unwin, 1983), pp. 32ff.
3. Noel Keane, "Parental Rights and Infertility," unpublished manuscript, p. 8.
4. Kings 3:16–28.
5. Alan A. Rassaby, "Surrogate Motherhood: The position and problems of substitutes," in William A. W. Walters and Peter Singer, eds., *Test-Tube Babies* (Melbourne: Oxford University Press, 1982), p. 100.
6. George Annas, "Redefining Parenthood and Protecting Embryos: Why We Need New Laws," Hastings Center *Report* 14 (October 1984):51. This sentence is in italics in the original.
7. Ibid.
8. Ibid.
9. Oliver O'Donovan, *Begotten or Made?* (Oxford: Clarendon Press, 1984), p. 46.
10. Ibid. Emphasis in the original.
11. Ibid.
12. Ibid., p. 48. Emphasis in original
13. Ibid., p. 47.
14. For an elaboration of this position, see Robert G. Edwards and David J. Sharpe, "Social Values and Research in Human Embryology," *Nature* 231 (14 May 1971):87ff., and Peter Singer, "Response," *Journal of Medical Ethics* 9 (1983):199.
15. Leon Kass, "Making Babies—the New Biology and the 'Old' Morality," *Public Interest* 26 (Winter 1972):32ff.
16. Paul Ramsey, "Shall We Reproduce?: II," *Journal of the American Medical Association* 220 (12 June 1972):1485, n. 3.
17. Leon Kass, *Toward A More Natural Science* (New York: Free Press, 1985), p. 159.
18. In the following I am developing ideas suggested by Oliver O'Donovan in *Begotten or Made?*, pp. 67ff.

19. H. T. Englehardt, Jr., M.D., "Allocating Scarce Medical Resources and the Availability of Organ Transplantation," *New England Journal of Medicine* 311 (5 July 1984):66–71. This article highlights very nicely the problem of contingency and fairness.

20. Kelly L. Frey, "New Reproductive Technologies: The Legal Problem and a Solution," *Tennessee Law Review* 49 (1982): pp. 323ff. Confer also Robert P. S. Jansen, "Sperm and Ova as Property," *Journal of Medical Ethics* 11 (1985):123–26, and Teresa Iglesias, "In Vitro Fertilization: The Major Issues," *Journal of Medical Ethics* 18 (1984):32ff.

21. Assumedly, ova would fall into this category, though to my knowledge no one has yet been paid for an ovum. The model has been that of donation. Although techniques for ova retrieval and preservation are of recent vintage, it is interesting that males are paid for their sperm, the obtaining of which is painless, harmless, and probably pleasurable; women are assumed to be willing to donate their ova even though a surgical procedure is required to obtain them and hormonal treatment is frequently initiated to obtain as many ova as possible.

22. Teresa Iglesias, "In Vitro Fertilization: The Major Issues," p. 33.

23. I. Kant, *Groundwork of the Metaphysics of Morals* (New York: Harper & Row, 1964), p. 102.

24. Thomas H. Murray, "Who Owns the Body? On the Ethics of Using Human Tissue for Commercial Puposes," *IRB: A Review of Human Subjects Research* 8 (January/February 1986):3.

25. Ibid., p. 5.

26. Snowden et al., *Artificial Reproduction*, pp. 46ff.

27. Ibid., p. 47.

28. Ibid., p. 48.

29. Ibid., p. 50.

30. Ibid., p. 53. Emphasis in original.

31. John A. Henley, "IVF and the Human Family: Possible and likely consequences," in *Test-Tube Babies*, pp. 86–87.

32. Ibid., p. 86.

33. Herbert T. Krimmel, "The Case against Surrogate Parenting," Hastings Center *Report* 13 (October 1983):38.

34. Ibid.

35. John Robertson, "Surrogate Mothers: Not So Novel After All," p. 30.

36. Steven R. Gersz, "The Contract in Surrogate Motherhood: A Review of the Issues," *Law, Medicine, and Health Care* 12 (June 1984):110ff.

37. John Biggers, "In Vitro Fertilization, Embryo Culture, and Embryo Transfer in the Woman," Appendix: HEW Support of Research Involving Human In Vitro Fertilization and Embryo Transfer (Ethics Advisory Board, U.S. Government Printing Office, 1979).

38. Ibid., p. 32.

39. Ibid.

40. Ibid.

41. Ibid., pp. 33–34.

42. John Biggers, "In Vitro Fertilization and Embryo Transfer in Human Beings," *New England Journal of Medicine* 304 (5 February 1981):341.

43. Clifford Gorbstein et al., "External Human Fertilization: An Evaluation of Policy," *Science* 222 (14 October 1983):128.

44. Ibid.

45. Ibid.

46. Ibid., p. 129. Confer also Barbara Menning, "In Defense of In Vitro Fertilization," in Helen Holmes, Betty B. Hoskins, and Michael Gross, *The Custom-Made Child* (Clifton, NJ: Humana Press, 1981), p. 264.

47. Paul Ramsey, *Fabricated Man: The Ethics of Genetic Control* (New Haven: Yale University Press, 1970), pp. 104ff. In the sixteen years since this book was first published, Ramsey has not changed his mind about this. His position prohibits not only the IVF procedure but also the research necessary to determine whether or not the procedure is safe. Ramsey's position is based on his understanding of the fertilized egg as a human person.

48. Leon Kass, " 'Making Babies' Revisited," *Public Interest* 54 (Winter 1979):32–60.

49. David T. Ozar, "The Case Against Thawing Unused Frozen Embryos," Hastings Center *Report* 15 (August 1985):11.

50. Oliver O'Donovan, *Begotten Or Made?*, p. 82.

51. Ibid., p. 83.

52. John Robertson, "Surrogate Mothers: Not So Novel After All," pp. 29ff. Confer also R. Snowden and G. D. Mitchell, *The Artificial Family* (London: George Allen and Unwin, 1981). This book is one of the few studies of the impact of AID on the parents.

53. Gena Corea, *The Mother Machine* (New York: Harper & Row, 1985), pp. 173–74.

54. LeRoy Walters, "Ethical Issues in Human In Vitro Fertilization and Research Involving Early Human Embryos," Appendix: HEW Support of Research Involving Human In Vitro Fertilization and Em-

bryo Transfer (Ethics Advisory Board, U.S. Government Printing Office, 4 May 1979), 1-p. 18.

55. Noel Keane, "Legal Problems of Surrogate Motherhood," *Southern Illinois University Law Journal*, 1980, p. 163. Emphasis added.

56. Emily Culpepper, quoted in *The Custom-Made Child?*, p. 276.

57. Ruth Hubbard, "The Case Against In Vitro Fertilization and Implantation," in *The Custom-Made Child?*, pp. 260ff.

58. Sharon M. Steeves, "Artificial Human Reproduction: Legal Problems Presented by the Test Tube Baby," *Speciality Law Digest: Health Care*, September 1981, pp. 12–13.

59. *Buck v. Bell* 274 U.S. 200 (1927) and *Skinner v. Oklahoma* 316 U.S. 535 (1942).

60. Kathryn V. Lorio, "In Vitro Fertilization and Embryo Transfer: Fertile Areas for Litigation," *Southwestern Law Journal* 35 (1982):1006–8.

61. Robertson, "Surrogate Mothers: Not so Novel After All," p. 32.

62. Noel Keane, "Legal Problems of Surrogate Mothers," p. 161.

63. 410 U.S. 113 (1973).

64. Steeves, "Artificial Human Reproduction," pp. 19–20.

65. Lorio, "In Vitro Fertilization," p. 1008.

66. Steeves, "Artificial Human Reproduction," p. 20, and Lorio, "In Vitro Fertilization," p. 1008.

67. "Protection of Human Subjects," Ethics Advisory Board, *Federal Register* 44, no. 118. (18 June 1979):35057.

68. Mark Evans et al., "Human In Vitro Fertilization," *Obstetrical and Gynecological Survey* 35 (1980):77. Emphasis in original.

69. Theresa M. Mady, "Surrogate Mothers: The Legal Issues," *American Journal of Law and Medicine* 7 (Fall 1981):329. Confer also Steven R. Gersz, "The Contract in Surrogate Motherhood: A Review of the Issues," *Law, Medicine and Health Care* 12 (June 1984):109ff.

70. John Robertson, "Surrogate Mothers: Not So Novel After All," p. 33.

71. Gersz, "The Contract in Surrogate Motherhood," p. 109. Confer also Noel Keane, "Parental Rights and Infertility," pp. 3–4.

72. Ibid.

73. Mady, "Surrogate Mothers: The Legal Issues," p. 332.

74. Alan A. Rassaby, "Surrogate Motherhood: The Position and Problems of Substitutes," in *Test-Tube Babies*, p. 104.

75. Keane, "Parental Rights and Infertility," p. 6.

76. Ibid.

77. Ibid.

78. Philip Parker, "The Psychology of the Pregnant Surrogate Mother: A Newly Updated Report of a Longitudinal Pilot Study," p. 5.

79. Angela Holder, "Surrogate Motherhood: Babies for Fun and Profit," *Law, Medicine and Health Care* 12 (June 1984):115. Holder also notes that in some jurisdictions even payment of hospital expenses is considered as akin to the sale of a baby.

80. Herbert Krimmell, "The Case Against Surrogate Parenting," Hastings Center *Report* 13 (October 1983):36.

81. Ibid.

82. Holder, "Surrogate Motherhood: Having Babies for Fun and Profit," p. 115.

83. Ibid.

84. Lindsey E. Harris, "Artificial Insemination and Surrogate Motherhood—A Nursery Full of Unrelsoved Questions," *Willamette Law Review* 17 (Fall 1981):345.

85. Holder, "Surrogate Motherhood: Selling Babies for Fun and Profit," p. 117. But given the fact that this contract is typically entered into before conception, the argument begs the question about the status of the fertilized egg if one reads *Roe* v. *Wade* seriously here. However, when the contract is fulfilled—when the child is transferred to the adopting parent(s), it is recognized as a human being and thus would fall under the terms of the Thirteenth Amendment. Nonetheless, there is some tension here about the status of the previable fetus.

86. Quoted in Corea, *The Mother Machine*, p. 277.

87. Ibid., p. 228. Confer also Andrea Dworkin, *Right-Wing Women* (New York: Coward-McCann, Inc., 1983), pp. 182ff.

88. Dworkin, *Right-Wing Women*, p. 182.

89. In an interesting dissent on the use of third parties in artificial reproduction, one member of the Ethics Committee of the American Fertility Society notes the following: "if the moral right to be inseminated by the sperm of another man is conceded, wives might easily conclude (and it would be difficult to reject their logic) that it is preferable (certainly more convenient and far less expensive) to be inseminated in the natural way. Thus, adulteries might be multiplied, to the detriment of marriage." The Ethics Committee of the American Fertility Society, "Ethical Considerations of the New Reproductive Technologies," *Fertility and Sterility*, 46 (September 1986):82s.

90. Susan E. Simanek, "Adoption Records Reform: Impact on Adoptees," *Marquette Law Review* 67 (1983):118ff.

91. G. G. Mitchell, "*In Vitro* Fertilization: the major issues—a comment," *Journal of Medical Ethics* 9 (1983):197.

92. George Annas and Sherman Elias, "*In Vitro* Fertilization and Embryo Transfer: Medicolegal Aspects of a New Technique to Create a Family," *Family Law Quaterly* 17 (Summer 1983):219ff.

93. The Ethics Committee for the American Fertility Society discusses this issue and its problems in its comments about the patent application for the uterine lavage technique ("Ethical Considerations," p. 47s).

94. Noel Keane, "Legal Problems of Surrogate Motherhood," p. 156.

95. George Annas, "Redefining Parenthood and Protecting Embryos: Why We Need New Laws," p. 14.

96. Ibid., p. 67.

97. Ibid.

98. Holder, "Surrogate Motherhood: Babies for Fun and Profit," p. 115.

99. Elizabeth Kolbert, "Battle for Baby M: Fierce Emotions and Key Legal Issues," *New York Times*, 23 August 1986, p. 25.

100. André Hellegers and Richard McCormick, "Unanswered Questions on Test Tube Life," *America* 39 (12 August 1979):77.

101. Krimmell, "The Case Against Surrogate Parenting," p. 38.

102. Holder, "Surrogate Motherhood: Babies for Fun and Profit," p. 115.

103. Ibid., p. 116.

104. Elizabeth Kolbert, "Battle for Baby M: Fierce Emotions and Key Legal Issues," p. 25.

105. Elizabeth Kolbert, "Baby M to Stay in Father's Care Pending Ruling," *New York Times*, 11 September 1986, p. B3.

106. John L. Morgan, "The Created Individual: Are Basic Notions of Humanity Threatened?," in William A. W. Walters and Peter Singer, *Test-Tube Babies*, pp. 89ff.

107. Dworkin, *Right-Wing Women*, p. 176 and p. 182.

108. Ibid., p. 183.

109. Corea, *The Mother Machine*, pp. 285ff.

110. Ibid., p. 290.

Chapter 5. The Regulation of Surrogate Motherhood

1. For the most recent overview of various international regulations, as well as a comparative study of them, see the special supplement to the Hastings Center *Report*, "Biomedical Ethics: A Multinational View," 17 (June 1987), Supplement, pp. 1–36. For the most current view of proposed state regulations, see Lori Andrews, "The Aftermath of Baby

M: Proposed State Laws on Surrogate Motherhood," Hastings Center *Report* 17 (October/November 1987):31–40.

2. The material in this chapter is not intended as a legal interpretation of various cases or regulations. I simply intend to present summaries or indications of the direction of courts or regulatory bodies. The material is, therefore, not to be construed as legal advice, but as an indication of current directions.

3. Lori Andrews, *New Conceptions* (New York: Ballantine Books, 1984), pp. 236–37.

4. Peter Singer and Deane Wells have provided a major service by collecting the available guidelines on artificial reproduction in their *Making Babies: The New Science and Ethics of Conception* (New York: Charles Scribner's Sons, 1985).

5. Ibid., pp. 191–92.

6. Ibid., p. 193.

7. Ibid., pp. 196–97.

8. Ibid., p. 198.

9. Ibid.

10. Ibid., p. 201.

11. Mary Warnock, *A Question of Life* (New York: Basil Blackwell, Ltd., 1985), pp. 44ff.

12. Ibid., p. 47.

13. Wendy Greengross and David Davies, "Expression of Dissent: A. Surrogacy," in Warnock, *A Question of Life*, p. 88.

14. Ibid., p. 89.

15. Ibid., p. 32.

16. Singer and Wells, *Making Babies*, p. 185.

17. For a listing of such statutes, confer the *ABA Journal*, August 1984.

18. William J. Curran, "Experimentation Becomes a Crime: Fetal Research in Massachusetts," *New England Journal of Medicine* 292 (6 February 1975):300–301. However, several IVF clinics are operating in Massachusetts and their existence can be understood as an interpretation of the legal situation there.

19. Uniform Parentage Act 5(b): The donor of semen provided for use in artificial insemination of a married woman other than the donor's wife is treated in law as if he were not the natural father of a child thereby conceived.

20. Andrews, *New Conceptions*, p. 206.

21. 313 U.S. 535 (1942).

22. 381 U.S. 479 (1965).

23. 405 U.S. 438 (1972).

24. 431 U.S. 685 (1977).
25. 410 U.S. 113 (1973).
26. 132 N.E. 2d 34 (1956).
27. 350 p. 2d 1 (1960).
28. Michigan Civil Action, No. 78 815 531 CZ. This can also be found in Noel Keane, *The Surrogate Mother* (New York: Everest House, 1981), pp. 336ff.
29. Keane, *The Surrogate Mother*, p. 340.
30. Ibid., p. 341.
31. Ibid., p. 342.
32. Ibid. Emphasis in original.
33. Ibid., pp. 342–45.
34. 333 N.W. 2d 209.
35. Ibid., p. 90.
36. Ibid., p. 93.
37. Ibid., p. 94.
38. 307 N.W. 2d 438 and 459 U.S. 1183.
39. Ibid., p. 441.
40. 704 S.W. 2d 209.
41. 704 S.W. 2d 210.
42. KRS 199.590(2), amended in 1984.
43. Ibid., p. 211.
44. Ibid., p. 214.
45. 505 N.Y.S. 2d 813.
46. Ibid.
47. 525 *Atlantic Reporter* 2d 1128 (N.J. Super. Ch., 1987).
48. Alan Grosman, "Surrogate Mothers, Failed Contracts," *United States Family Law News*, October 1986, p. 11.
49. Paula Span, "Couple, surrogate mother battle over the infant she bore," *Evening Gazette*, Worcester, MA, 21 October 1986, pp. 18–19.
50. 525 *Atlantic Reporter*, 2d 1163.
51. Shortly after the decision, the Whiteheads announced their separation, Mrs. Whitehead's pregnancy by a new partner, and their subsequent marriage after the divorce from Mr. Whitehead was completed.
52. *Evening Telegram*, Worcester, MA, 16 September 1987, p. 6.
53. *Family Law Reporter*, p. 2008.
54. Ibid., p. 2016.
55. Ibid.
56. Ibid., p. 2020. Emphasis in original.
57. Ibid., p. 2012.

58.   Ibid., p. 2017. Emphasis in original.

59.   Its two most significant cases were that of Karen Ann Quinlan and Claire Conroy.

60.   "Ethical Issues in Surrogate Motherhood," American College of Obstetricians and Gynecologists, 600 Maryland Ave, SW, Suite 300 East, Washington, DC, 20024.

61.   Given the current reading of *Roe* v. *Wade*, a surrogate's attempt to procure an abortion during the first two trimesters would be an interesting case to test the validity of the surrogacy contract and would provide additional insight into the moral and legal status of the embryo/ fetus. Can a contract override a constitutional right to privacy which neither the state nor anyone else has a right to restrain?

62.   "Ethical Issues in Surrogate Motherhood."

63.   Ibid.

64.   *Fertility and Sterility* 46 (September 1986), Supplement I.

65.   A fatal flaw in the whole report, in my judgment, is the contradiction between a general principle—that the procedures are to be offered "only if they provide a reasonable chance of solving the *medical* problem" (p. v, emphasis added). If the medical problem is infertility, the reproductive technologies do not resolve that problem and thus violate a major premise of the whole process of justification. The reproductive technologies resolve childlessness, not infertility. If infertile before IVF, ET, preembryonic lavage, or surrogacy, the individual is still infertile. Thus the report avoids coming to grips with a critical problem: In what sense do the reproductive technologies fit into the traditional medical model.

66.   Ibid., pp. 58s–59s. In this section I will simply summarize the content of the report and note where the information can be located in the next rather than provide extensive quotations from it. When giving the actual recommendations, I will quote from the report.

67.   Ibid., pp. 59s–60s.

68.   This is defined in the report as "an innovative precedure that has a very limited or no historical record of whether any success can be achieved." Ibid., p. vii.

69.   Ibid., p. 61s.

70.   Ibid.

71.   Ibid.

72.   Ibid., p. 63s.

73.   Ibid., p. 64s.

74.   Ibid.

75.   Ibid., p. 67s. Although this statement claims that surrogacy is a medical solution to infertility, it is actually a medical solution for the

psychosocial problem of childlessness. The causes of infertility have not been dealt with.

Chapter 6. Conclusions

1. William F. May, "Religion and the Donation of Body Parts," *Hastings Center Report* 15 (February 1985):38–42.

2. Marx Wartofsky, "On Doing It for Money," Thomas A. Mappes and Jane S. Zembaty, eds, *Biomedical Ethics* (New York: McGraw-Hill, 1981), pp. 186–94.

3. Thomas H. Murray, "Who Owns the Body? On the Ethics of Using Human Tissue for Commercial Purposes," *IRB: A Review of Human Subjects Research* 8 (January/February 1986):3.

4. Andrea Dworkin, *Right-Wing Women* (New York: Coward-McCann, Inc., 1983), pp. 176 and 182.

5. Judith Blake, "Coercive Pronatalism and American Population Policy," in E. Peck and J. Senderowitz, eds, *Pronatalism: The Myth of Mom and Apple Pie* (New York: Thomas Y. Crowell Company, 1974), pp. 29–67.

6. Philip Parker, M.D., "Motivation of Surrogate Mothers: Initial Findings," *American Journal of Psychiatry* 140 (January 1983):117.

7. Angela Holder, quoted in Iver Peterson, "Ruling in Baby M Case is Due Today," *New York Times*, 31 March 1987, p. B2

8. Noel Keane, "Legal Problems of Surrogate Motherhood," *Southern Illinois University Law Journal*, 1980, p. 156.

9. Angela Holder, "Surrogate Motherhood: Babies for Fun and Profit," *Law, Medicine, and Health Care* 12 (June 1984):115–17.

10. Kathryn V. Lorio, "In Vitro Fertilization and Embryo Transfer: Fertile Areas for Litigation," *Southwest Law Journal* 35 (1982):1006ff. John Robertson, "Procreative Liberty and the Control of Conception, Pregnancy, and Childbirth," *Virginia Law Review* 69 (April 1983):405–63.

11. H. Tristram Engelhardt, Jr., M.D., Ph.D., "Allocating Scarce Medical Resources and the Availability of Organ Transplantation," *New England Journal of Medicine* 311 (5 July 1984):68.

Index

187